JOHN LEY-MORGAN was
Somerset in 1938. He read
after a 5-year Short Service Commission in the Royal Navy, taught for 30 years in the Bristol area. Taking early retirement in 1993, he enrolled at the University of the West of England to read law and then practiced as a solicitor for a further 12 years. He is a local councillor, a past mayor of WsM and his hobbies include family history research. He is also new to beekeeping.

ANNE LEY-MORGAN was born in London in 1954 but her family soon moved to her mother's home town of Exmouth, Devon. She trained as a PE teacher at Bedford College before starting her first job at Backwell, Somerset where she met John. She then managed her own small hotel in North Devon before opening a health food shop and restaurant in Weston which ran successfully for 14 years. Anne returned to full-time teaching in 2000 and currently works at a local comprehensive where she teaches Food Technology and Child Development.

Published in by SilverWood Books 2010

www.silverwoodbooks.co.uk

ISBN 978-1-906236-40-4 (paperback edition)
ISBN 978-1-906236-41-0 (hardback edition)

British Library Cataloguing in Publication Data
A CIP catalogue record for this book is available from the British Library

Set in Palatino by SilverWood Books
Printed in England by The Short Run Press
on paper certified as being from sustainable sources

Cover image: Ellie, Ha Long Bay 2004

ELLIE

Rainbow's End

John and Anne Ley-Morgan

A voyage of discovery and love

SilverWood

This book is dedicated to our daughter, Ellen Frances Vu Duong Ley-Morgan – universally known as Ellie – born 1st November 1995 in a rural community in the north of Vietnam, not far from Hanoi.

Ellie filled and continues to fill a massive hole in our lives and we hope that she will treasure this book which is an attempt to explain how we became a family.

However, this account would not be complete without an acknowledgement of all the tremendous help and encouragement we received from my sister, Gill Sweet, and Margaret Daly in the UK and Nguyen Chien and Vu Anh in Hanoi. Without their help and support our quest would have been so much more difficult, if not impossible.

But our greatest thanks and gratitude must go to Sue Loveday without whose advice, experience and help this whole adventure would never have got off the ground let alone arrived at a successful and wonderful conclusion.

It is sometimes said that it is better to travel than to arrive. That is not necessarily so. We travelled a rocky and painful journey over many years but the arrival was far sweeter than we could ever have imagined. Hopefully, other couples who may find themselves in a similar position will be encouraged to carry on to the end of their own particular rainbow.

John Ley-Morgan
Weston-super-Mare
Somerset
October 2009

Contents

Ellie's middle name, Vu Du'o'ng, is actually the name of her village and was given to her by her birth parents to take away as a permanent reminder of, and connection to, her origins.

We decided to retain it as part of her name – although the overall result is rather a mouthful for someone who is always going to be quite small!

1

The Return

John
Tuesday 20th July 2004

It has been a long time in the planning but here we are, at last, on the flight path into Noi Bai, Hanoi's Airport in the north of Vietnam.

We have deliberately waited until Ellie is old enough to understand what she will be seeing, and to appreciate how the Vietnamese people live – her birth family in particular. How different her life is and has been from theirs over the past eight years.

To be honest, we hope that Ellie will consider her home life and conditions in England so superior to her birth family's in Vietnam that this visit will reinforce rather than weaken her bonds with us.

It has been very much easier to plan for this trip than for our first visit in 1996. For a start, we have had so much longer to prepare and we have only had ourselves to think about. The timetable has been ours to organise – complicated only by the fact that after ten days in Vietnam we will be going on to Australia for a further four weeks to visit friends and distant relatives. Away for six weeks in all, two different sets of clothes to pack for two different climates…

Ellie's original Vietnamese passport, issued at the age of three months, has long since been replaced by a British one but visas had to be applied for to enter both Vietnam and, to our surprise, Australia. Various inoculations to organise, flights and hotels to be booked and US and Australian dollars and travellers cheques arranged.

We had unhesitatingly decided to fly Singapore Airlines again – surely one of the best in the world – and they had generously increased our luggage allowance when I told them that we were taking with us various items for the village school. In fact, they had doubled our allowance and, consequently, as well as our suitcases for a six week stay away from home, we had three large blue polystyrene boxes crammed full of exercise books, pens, pencils, crayons, paints, jigsaw puzzles *et cetera* – all donated by family, friends and work colleagues.

Yesterday, Anne's brother, Ian, had driven the three of us in our car from our home in Weston-super-Mare to the airport at London Heathrow. Our suitcases filled the boot and I had taken out the front passenger seat to make room to pile the blue boxes. Anne, Ellie and I sat in the back. Even then it was a bit of a squeeze – but nothing like we were to experience later when we arrived in Hanoi!

The flight to Singapore seemed shorter this time and Anne and I were frequently saying to each other, "Do you remember…" as our journey brought back so many memories of our previous trip in January 1996. The in-flight entertainment was more sophisticated with a long catalogue of films available to watch on a small screen set into the back of the seat in front of each of us. Earphones added a choice of language. None of us slept during any part of the journey. Never were so many films watched by so few!

Certainly that entertainment helped to pass the time and the twelve-hour journey Heathrow-Singapore (surely it was fourteen hours last time?) passed relatively quickly. Around us other passengers slept but none of the three of us seemed capable of doing the same. The plane's flight path was shown on a map at the front of our compartment and we monitored the screen from time to time as the line extended over Belgium, Holland, Germany, Poland and Ukraine before heading across the northern tip of the Black Sea and into Georgian air space. Onwards across the northern tip of the Caspian Sea and then over some of the 'stans' – Kazakhstan, Uzbekistan, north west tip of Afghanistan and north west Pakistan before cutting diagonally across northern India and out over the Bay of Bengal. We crossed the north-west tip of Thailand before flying the length of Malaysia and, finally, down into Singapore.

A four-hour stopover, a change of plane and we were off again. Neither Anne nor I can resist giving Ellie intermittent geography lessons from the flight path monitor but she is more interested in watching Shrek 2! It is morning during this leg of the journey on Day 2 and Anne and I take every opportunity to try to glimpse the ground below. The map on the bulkhead at the front of our section of this much smaller plane again shows our flight path as we cross the southern tip of Cambodia and the Mekong Delta – its muddy waters visible through the window – before flying the length of Vietnam to our destination, the northern capital of Hanoi, not far from the border with China.

And now we are coming in to land with over eight thousand air miles behind us. This time, Vietnamese peasants are not farming right up to the edge of the runway as they were in 1996. What other changes will we see?

As we disembark it is immediately noticeable that the humidity is high despite a gentle rain. It is a relief to get into the terminal building itself and, another surprise, it is brand new with a very efficient air conditioning system. Some things have not changed, however, and after we have collected our baggage from the carousel we have to stand behind a line until called forward for passports to be examined. Even then, only I am allowed to cross the line to be dealt with by a non-smiling, seemingly unwelcoming official.

And then we are out onto the concourse and looking for a taxi to take us into Hanoi about ten miles away. We are not sure if the hotel has arranged for us to be met but two young men standing beside a four-seater saloon come forward and one hesitatingly introduces himself as an hotel employee.

When I said that the trip to Heathrow in our own car had been a squeeze it was nothing to what we were about to experience. Two extra adults (where there had previously been only Ian in our car), no extra room created by the removal of the front passenger seat... and no air-conditioning! But we all manage to lever ourselves in with the suitcases in the boot, Anne, Ellie and one of the young men in the back with the three blue boxes on their laps – and me in the front passenger seat so that I can film the journey into Hanoi with the camcorder. Lucky me!

More changes are quickly noticeable – hardly surprising, I suppose, after an eight and a half year gap. Public transport in the form of single-decker, red-and-yellow buses is much in evidence along the road; many more cars where previously we had seen only the occasional official car in 1996. The way is vaguely familiar and eventually we come into the outskirts of Hanoi, bump over the railway line (still no level crossing gates!) and stop at the end of the short road, now pedestrianised, containing the Dream 2 hotel.

The smiling manager is new but we had been corresponding by email for several weeks and I feel a degree of familiarity with him. His English is limited but adequate – far better than my non-existent command of the Vietnamese language.

We had asked for the same room we occupied for five and a half weeks in 1996 but, apparently, it is not available until tomorrow. We are escorted to another hotel about four hundred yards away taking just one suitcase with essentials. After a quick wash all three of us fall into bed and sleep soundly for a full twelve hours. Next day, after breakfast, we return to the Dream 2 hotel and are shown to our old room. Already, Ellie must be getting thoroughly fed up with Anne and I prefacing virtually every sentence with "Do you remember…?"

Even after eight and a half years it is very familiar with few changes. This time, however, we are in control, confident that we know perfectly well what this visit will entail.

How different it had been in 1996.

2

Two CVs

John Ley-Morgan
Born 19 May 1938 at Weston-super-Mare, Somerset.
Educated at the local Grammar School for Boys 1949-57.
National Service had been scrapped whilst I had tempo-
rary exemption as I underwent teacher training at St Luke's
College, Exeter – so, somewhat perversely, I went into the
Royal Navy in August 1960 on a five year Short Service
Commission in the Instructor Branch in the hope that
teachers' abysmal pay would improve in the meanwhile.

Within three and a half months I had met and married
a WREN with Mark (27 September 1961) and Frances (9
October 1963) arriving in reasonably short order. In 1965
I left the Navy for a teaching post in the Preparatory of a
minor public school in Bromsgrove, near Birmingham. In
1967 I applied for and was appointed to the post of second
in the mathematics department at Bristol Cathedral School
(BCS), a small Direct Grant Grammar School for boys. We
bought our first house in the village of Portbury in Somerset, just a few miles south of Isambard Kingdom Brunel's
famous Bristol Suspension Bridge.

Five years later, the opportunity for further promotion and a slight change of direction presented itself when I successfully applied for a position as a Head of House at Backwell School, a large 11-18 comprehensive between Weston-super-Mare and Bristol. The post enabled me to continue teaching mathematics to A level whilst opening the way to developing a career on the pastoral side and in schools administration – hopefully a move towards an eventual appointment as a senior teacher, deputy head or even, maybe, a headship itself in the fullness of time. Looking back, those years at BCS and Backwell were golden times. Great kids, few disciplinary problems, supportive parents and considerable job satisfaction.

Many so-called high-fliers in teaching spend a year or two in a succession of different posts and are deemed to be hugely experienced whereas I reckon I refined and improved the way I tackled most aspects of the job of Head of House year after year. But, looking back, I realise that I could not have been particularly ambitious. I was doing a job I enjoyed but my real life's project was my family.

My wife and I were from totally different backgrounds and although we made 'a handsome couple' there were underlying tensions that emanated from our different outlooks on life. Money was always a bit of a problem as we had only my income; I had come from a savings culture whereas if Andrea had a pound in her pocket she could not wait to spend it in half a dozen different ways. That is not intended to be a criticism. It is just the way we were.

But we had produced two wonderful children. Mark was always responsive to encouragement and mature beyond his years. By the time he was ten he had won a scholarship to Bristol Cathedral School – one of only ten 10-year olds amongst an intake of sixty otherwise 11-year olds. He started at BCS in the autumn of 1972, the term after I had left to go to Backwell.

Two years later, Frances also gained a scholarship, this time to Red Maids, another of Bristol's Direct Grant Grammar Schools.

But, soon afterwards, in the summer of 1975, problems came to a head at home and I returned from work one day to find my wife had gone. A goodbye note and her wedding ring on the bookcase in the hallway said it all.

I subsequently discovered that she had been having an affair for a number of months with a former neighbour and they had both left their families to set up home together.

My world collapsed, my 'life project' apparently in tatters. But I was determined to keep the children with me and for their lives and mine to continue with as much normality as possible. I had to learn a variety of new skills in a very short space of time: shopping, cooking, washing, ironing – the Open University degree I was three years into had to be modified to a less ambitious programme. What a lot of time I had previously wasted crashed in front of a TV set!

Portbury villagers were remarkably supportive but, even so, many of them expressed surprise when the courts subsequently awarded me custody of both children. It did not – and still does not – usually happen like that for fathers. Ask Fathers for Justice!

Then came the summer holidays and a little respite before the new school year started in September. Amongst new members of staff at Backwell was an entire Girls' PE department – Katie, Cae and Anne. Keen for some adult company I went out with Katie two or three times and once or twice with Anne. On one of those occasions I ran out of petrol within a couple of hundred yards. Anne must have doubted my intentions!

With some accumulated back pay I had previously

arranged for and paid for the whole family to join the school's annual Christmas ski trip to Austria. With my wife no longer using her place and keen to try to recoup my loss, I asked Anne if she would be interested in joining the trip. She said that she was – and it was during that holiday that we came to recognise a mutual attraction.

Anne moved in with Mark, Frances and me early in the new year.

Anne Ley-Morgan née Curryer

Thinking back to my life before John, it followed a predictable but not always easy pattern. My family moved to Exmouth, Devon (mother's home town) from London in 1961 when I was only five years old and after my father's breakdown. This had had, and continued to have, a devastating effect on the family. With the support of a vast array of aunts and uncles and other relatives we were able to cope as a family and to buy a small terraced house in Lawn Road that became the first home we had ever owned. What a change of lifestyle this proved to be for three streetwise kids with marked cockney accents. A real turning point for us all. Dad's continuing illness and eventual diagnosis of schizophrenia was ever present but rarely discussed between my two older brothers and me. It formed a dark shadow in an otherwise idyllic life where we all had the chance to grow independently in a world where children were largely unsupervised.

Since Dad was never able to work again, our meagre income of benefits and Mum's wages from several cleaning jobs made us all aware of the value of money. From an early age we learnt that if we wanted something we had to save and buy it ourselves, a philosophy sadly lacking in today's world. I loathed and detested the system that forced me to hand in a ticket for my free school meals, marking me out as different from other children. A chance win of £25 on premium bonds (given to me by my grandmother) was seen by me as an immediate opportunity to purchase the school uniform worn by everyone else at Primary School. How today's children would wonder at such an idea!

During this time Mum became the mainstay of our family as Dad yo-yo'd between home and hospital until his eventual sad and undeserved death in 1971 from stomach cancer. Since he had always been the love of her life this was a true tragedy for Mum and the great esteem we all three hold her in stems from acknowledging how well she coped throughout this period. She was successfully able to bring us up single-handed, achieving her aim of giving us as normal a life as possible.

Following 6th form and Bedford P.E. College, my first teaching job was at Backwell Comprehensive School between Weston-super-Mare and Bristol. I remember meeting John during my interview in early June when we exchanged some witty repartee and this formed the basis of our totally platonic relationship when I began teaching at the school in September 1975. John was part of the senior staff at the school, not only coping with a demanding job but also going through a great deal in his personal life since his wife of fourteen years had left him in the previous June. Surprisingly, John had subsequently gained custody of both children, Mark aged 14 and Frances 12, an unusual occurrence at that time and something he had fought hard to achieve. I was proud to recognise his commitment to them which showed a depth beyond the flippant attitude he liked to exhibit.

Earlier in the year John had received some back pay and the family democratically decided how they wished to spend the money. The overwhelming vote was to join the school ski trip going to Italy just after Christmas, despite

John's preference for a colour TV! With the departure of his wife and mindful of losing the money already paid, John offered the place to me. It was an opportunity I jumped at and I was excited at the prospect of an activity holiday. My boyfriend of five years was none too happy since it meant me going away on Boxing Day but I gave little thought to his objections. Our relationship had reached a plateau and seemed to be going nowhere. I had been happy to take a job near Bristol whilst he had already secured one in London, using the excuse that I couldn't possibly teach in London (which probably, for me, was true!). We had been through many things together, including the deaths of both our fathers and I was reluctant to cut my ties with the past although I could not acknowledge this even to myself.

During the trip the casual friendship John and I had previously experienced as colleagues changed suddenly and overwhelmingly and I had to admit to myself that I was head over heels in love. This was the start of a new era for us both when we were reluctant to be apart and delighted in the effect we had on each other. To my shame, on our return I quickly informed my boyfriend what had happened but felt I owed him no less than the truth. Within a few months, to the horror and opposition of my family I had moved in with John, reacting in an impetuous manner that was so uncharacteristic of my normal behaviour. It was also totally contrary to the views and opinions I had regarding relationships and marriage and so was an enormous thing for me to do. I knew this was a big decision and that it would not be easy, particularly coping with two children of the ages of Mark and Frances but it was simply the next logical and inevitable step in our relationship. I quickly brushed aside any doubts I may have had since our desire to be together was so great and left us nowhere else to go.

3

A New Life Together

John

It was a very tall order for a 21 year old to be suddenly faced with a ready-made family. I was 37 years old, Mark 14 years and Frances 12 years but Anne coped very well – within limits! Mark was his fairly amenable self but Frances would often be difficult which, perhaps, Anne as the older person could have handled better. I sometimes felt like the piggy-in-the-middle not wanting to be seen to be taking sides.

My divorce went through but eventually Frances, who had been spending more and more weekends with her mother, went to live with her permanently. It was, unfortunately, the beginning of a gradual distancing between Frances and me and she does not want to see me these days. This is a bitter disappointment for me as I love her dearly and, additionally, I never get to see my eldest grandchild, Harry.

But life certainly became that little bit easier for Anne and we were married soon afterwards in her home town of Exmouth on 12 April 1977.

* * *

I began to apply to other schools for posts as senior teacher and deputy headships but although I was short-listed for some, interviews were few and far between. My Heads of House colleagues were experiencing the same problems until one of them was told by a County Adviser that we were on the wrong salary scale to warrant serous considerations. Heads of House in other schools were on a higher grade than us whilst having only part of our responsibilities but our subsequent representations to the Head fell on deaf ears.

Within a short space of time all four of us had moved on in other directions, two into their subject areas, one a sideways move as a Head of House on a different salary grade in another part of the country – and me to North Devon as an hotelier!

The thought of moving out of teaching began to take shape but what to do when you've got no tried-and-tested skills? I was good at organising and had been secretary of the local rugby club, treasurer and chief fundraiser for the local cricket club and a leading light in the development and running of functions at the Portbury village hall but I could not see a new career flourishing from these particular acorns. Keith Garland was a colleague at Backwell School and his wife, Jean, and Anne had formed an early and very close bond and friendship. With three boys of her own, perhaps Jean looked on Anne as the daughter she had never had. Jean had a background in catering – something that Anne had an interest in and flair for. When the Garlands bought a small hotel in Cheddar, Jean and Anne worked closely together with Anne learning valuable tips of the trade. Both of us were still teaching at that time.

So Anne and I started to search for a suitable place of our own – ideally somewhere between Bristol and

Plymouth, an area we both liked, felt we knew well and a popular West Country holiday destination. Mark was now in his second year at University and was likely to move on once he had qualified. He was already talking of taking time out to travel once he had graduated. My father had died recently and with his modest legacy divided between my sister, Gill, and me and with the net proceeds of the sale of my house in Portbury, Anne and I were able to buy a nine-bedroom hotel in Ilfracombe, North Devon with the help of a five year business loan from the bank.

Unfortunately, our research had been defective! Whilst 'Sea View' (almost immediately renamed by us 'The Georgian House') was a very well-appointed and attractive property –in the middle of a Georgian terrace built in the early 1800s, we were told, from Napoleonic Wars prize money – the north Devon holiday season was short. Within a few months it was evident that our aim to work hard through the summer and, perhaps, winter in the sun was never going to be realised and it seemed only sensible for me to take a teaching post at a Barnstaple comprehensive straight from Backwell.

We ran The Georgian House for five years without really settling in the area. The repeat business we experienced showed that we were – or, rather, Anne was – doing a good job but it was not for us. Nevertheless, it gave us a degree of self and business confidence and the success of the local health food shop was the spur for us to look to open something similar if we could somewhere find a gap in the market. Once again, we were ideally looking for a place somewhere between Bristol and Plymouth – an area we both knew and loved. The sale of The Georgian House in 1986 enabled us to buy a property on the outskirts of Weston-super-Mare – which just happened, coincidentally, to be my home town – where The Corn Dolly was created from scratch as a health food shop with café attached. The self-contained one-bedroom flat over became our new home. It was a very comfortable move for us both. Additionally, we were back amongst friends.

Soon, Anne had a loyal band of part-time staff in place to assist her and I, as the supernumerary, took another teaching post at a local comprehensive school. Anne was soon able to leave her Corn Dollies to run the business whilst she took employment as a supply teacher at another local school. This connection eventually led, as we shall see and some seventeen years later, to her being appointed as a permanent member of staff.

Around early 1986, some of Anne's old school and college friends started having children and, although she never spoke about it, I began to wonder if Anne was beginning to regret the absence of a family of her own. In the last year of my marriage I had had a vasectomy as the 'big gesture' to my wife who had made it plain that she did not want any more children. In those days the operation was considered irreversible and Anne was aware of this when we married. I had my family and had considered myself too old to start again but, privately, I began to question that decision in my mind and eventually concluded that it had been a selfish one. Anne had always been (and still is) very slow to express her feelings but she immediately responded positively to my suggestion that I should try to have the vasectomy reversed.

Was I mad? Too old to start another family at 38 when we married but now actively considering the possibility at 50!!

My surgeon, Roger Fenelay, was very cautious about the chances of success but booked me into St. Mary's private hospital, Bristol. Within a comparatively short time I started to produce sperm but they were of low quality with poor mobility and the hoped-for pregnancy did not materialise.

In despair our thoughts then turned briefly to fostering. However, we rather soon concluded that we would be unable to become emotionally attached to a child only to give him or her up after the appropriate period.

We enquired about adoption and were visited by a social worker from Avon County Council, the local authority at that time. It was immediately evident that at our ages – me 50 years old, Anne 34 years – a baby was out of the question. Older or disabled children were available – subject to our perceived suitability – but whilst these would have been considered at a later stage we both wanted Anne to have a baby in the first instance.

In 1991 we moved to our present home in Elmsleigh Road, Weston-super-Mare – an imposing, double-fronted five-bedroom property built around 1917. It was the sort of property neither of us had previously thought we would ever own – a most attractive house with a large garden in a quiet area of town. Absolutely begging to be used again as a home for a family. I now felt the need to have one last attempt and, in October 1991, I was back at St Mary's for Roger Fenelay to attempt a second reversal. In resulting tests I was unable to produce any sperm and so another door appeared to have closed in our faces.

We then started down the road to infertility treatments – IVF.

4

IVF and All That…

Our family doctor, Richard Darling, at the Worle Surgery was hugely supportive and referred us to St Michael's Hospital in Bristol. Every month for a year, from November 1992 to August 1993, we went for Anne to be treated with donor sperm. I drove her home whilst insisting that she lay flat in the reclined passenger seat with her feet on the dashboard lest gravity conspire to defeat us! We knew the odds were not on our side either but, optimistically, hoped that each month might shorten them in our favour. A spinning coin cannot come down tails forever but disappointments were accumulating month after month – especially when Anne was overdue by a day or two only for her period to crush our expectations. The memory of Anne's distress after one particular failure brings tears to my eyes even now.

(Our basic instinct was supported in 2009 when a Dutch study of four hundred couples discovered that lying down for ten minutes after artificial insemination could increase the chances of a successful pregnancy. The study, reported in the British Medical Journal, found that 27 per cent of women who lay down following insemination conceived, compared with 18 per cent of those who did not.)

After a year, and many hundreds of pounds out-of-pocket, we were referred to Southmead Hospital in Bristol for further tests. Unfortunately, free treatment was not available on the NHS since we lived outside the hospital's catchment area.

We were then referred to The Glen, a private hospital on the Downs at Bristol, the former site of *the* local night-club in my younger days as a teen-and-twenty in Weston.

Anne underwent further courses of treatment – four IVF and one GIFT – over the next eighteen months, a period even more intensely emotional than before. The additional drugs and nose sprays Anne required were provided under prescription by Richard Darling who was still supporting her to the extent of his ability for which we shall be forever grateful.

The monthly letdowns were difficult to bear for both of us. After expending some £12,000 we had the choice of carrying on with what seemed to be an increasingly forlorn hope, giving up and settling for a life without children or going back to the exploration of adoption.

It had been two years since our last contact with Social Services but we soon discovered that little had changed. We had a meeting at our home with one social worker who reiterated the local authority's policy that a full Home Study would be required with no guarantee that we would be found 'suitable'. The timetable was lengthy. I asked a few fairly simple questions which she was unable to answer there-and-then but she promised to get back to me. We waited for her to do so but, in the end, had to chase her six weeks later for replies. ("I do have other cases, Mr Ley-Morgan, and I've also been on holiday"). I felt like telling her that she clearly did not live in the real world

28

that we were inhabiting!

Here we were with a lovely home, a secure marriage, love in abundance and financially reasonably well-off whilst Social Services – no doubt well-meaning – seemed to prefer that children should remain in care rather than be placed with people like us. Mixed race children were out of the question as the powers-that-be wanted to protect their 'sense of identity' and would only place them with coloured or mixed-race families. Other people could have children of their own regardless of their suitability and regardless of whether they were in a stable relationship or not. Single people could adopt and homosexuals and lesbians but we were to be denied on the grounds of age. To my mind it was, and still is, political correction gone mad.

Time had never really been on our side and was now fast running out. Our thoughts turned to foreign adoption but Avon County Council still had a policy of not getting involved in such cases. We would have to deal with an Agency in London – a process likely to cost around £4,000 and take about two years with, again, no guarantees of acceptance or success.

By now, 1993, I had taken early retirement from teaching (after 33 years!) to take up a place at the University of the West of England (UWE) to read law. Mark, who had gained a BSc in Quantity Surveying at Portsmouth in 1983, had undertaken an external London University LLB course in the early 1990s and after qualifying, had resigned his job to pursue the one-year barrister's course at Gray's Inn, London. I think this spurred me – at 55 years of age – to try something similar. With my retirement lump sum, savings and Anne's support I set out on a two-year course at UWE that would give me the academic qualifications to practise as a solicitor. I qualified two years later and immediately commenced a two-year training contract (previously known as articles) with a small local firm in September 1995.

During this time the war in Bosnia was daily headline news on TV and in all the newspapers and suddenly we all heard of veteran war and award-winning chief foreign correspondent for ITN, Michael Nicholson, returning from war-torn Sarajevo with a young orphan girl whom he intended to adopt. The story mentioned that he lived in Hazlemere near High Wycombe in Buckinghamshire and the following morning I was on my way to try to pick his brains as to how we might go about bringing another child back to the UK.

I had no idea how to find him or exactly what I would say but a chance contact like this might never materialise again and I could not let the opportunity slip through my fingers.

After a high-speed drive up the M4 motorway I arrived in Hazlemere and stopped for directions. Mr Nicholson was obviously very well-known in the town and the first person I spoke to gave me directions to his house. I found it a few minutes later – the house out-of-sight down a curving driveway with a knot of what I assumed to be reporters and photographers clustered at the entrance. I parked a hundred yards down the road, walked back and without glancing left or right strode through them and headed up the drive. The front door was at the rear of the property and I knocked. No reply. Had I come all this way to miss him? On the drive from Weston I had tried to anticipate how any conversation might go but, somehow, I had been unable to rehearse exactly what I would say to Mr Nicholson. I decided to wait. I knocked again on the off chance that he was in, my heart in my mouth with nervousness.

A few moments later a voice above me called out and, stepping back, I saw Michael Nicholson leaning out of a first floor window. He was instantly recognisable since I had seen him on ITV News programmes on many occasions. Given the small crowd at the gateway, I had a sudden fear that he would assume that I was a reporter, give me short shrift and close the window on me. I haltingly introduced myself and briefly explained what I had come for. Could he help in any way – perhaps a contact name and telephone number? The window closed and I wondered if that was it. However, after a short wait, the front door opened and I was invited in by a slightly brusque Mr Nicholson who appeared to be about my age or a little older. He expressed doubts about his ability to help but went to his desk and quickly wrote down the names and telephone numbers of a couple of people in Sarajevo who he thought might be able to assist and then I was shown out. I was back in my car no more than ten minutes after I had left it and on my way back down the M4 to Weston. It was a long trip for such a brief encounter yet I felt enormously elated.

Michael Nicholson's contacts turned out not to be able to help and, anyway, by then Bosnia and the surrounding countries were closed to foreigners. It would have been far too dangerous to travel to an area where genocide and random killings were daily occurrences. Nevertheless, every avenue needed to be explored, every straw clutched at, no stone left unturned. Time continued to be our greatest enemy and lateral thinking was obviously required. By now, we were far too committed to give up and determination had set in.

At my suggestion – or, rather, at my insistence – Anne had begun writing to foreign embassies for details of their adoption policies. We soon discovered that the majority of countries – including China – had signed up to a protocol creating a reciprocal arrangement with the UK whereby potential adopters had to produce a UK Home

Study report. It seemed that we were back again faced with the only option of dealing with the agency in London with the attendant costs and delays that seemed to encompass. Additionally, there were absolutely no guarantees of success.

However, it then turned out that a few countries were not part of the protocol including Vietnam and some South American countries. Anne's letter of enquiry of the Vietnam Trade Delegation (they did not have an embassy, as such, in 1995) brought a compliment slip by way of reply.

And so Sue Loveday came into our lives – and changed it forever.

As Winston Churchill had said on a previous occasion, it was the end of the beginning.

5

From Anne's Perspective

Anne

Looking back to early 1976, I wonder how I coped since not only was I in my first year of a demanding new job but suddenly helping to run a home, a task I had no real experience of. The shambolic running of a student flat bore no comparison! It was hard for all of us for different reasons and I lacked the maturity to make allowances for the children's behaviour and their emotional needs, the age gap between us being not so great. Frances found it particularly challenging and, missing her mother, had, within a year, moved to live with her and her new partner. Nearly a year after I met John his divorce came through and we were eventually married in April 1977 – always remembered as the Queen's Silver Jubilee year. I had always wanted a church wedding but unfortunately John's divorce precluded this and we had to settle for the registry office in Exeter followed by a blessing at Withycombe Church, Exmouth where my mother had also been married. The ridiculous thing was that when we came to the actual ceremony it was so similar to a real wedding service that few people could have told the difference!

The next four years were a steep learning curve as I struggled to learn to share John with his children and to fit in all the demands of a hectic lifestyle. I was probably more moody during that time than at any other period of my life and looking back, with the benefit of hindsight, can appreciate the many mistakes I made! With the departure of Mark to Portsmouth Poly to start a three-year course leading to a BSc in Quantity Surveying we were finally on our own but were, by then, in the throes of changing our lives completely.

The death of John's father in late 1979 gave him a small legacy and the opportunity to rethink his priorities. The increasing difficulties involved in teaching in a changing social and politically correct world were things that particularly irritated John and he relished the prospect of a change of career. After only a few years in teaching I was happy, if not keen, to go along with this and we spent many hours reviewing our options. With few 'real world' skills that I was aware of except my interest in cooking, we decided that a small hotel might be the logical answer. A year of searching led us finally to The Georgian House Hotel in Ilfracombe (quickly renamed from the unimaginative 'Sea View') where we spent a hard, relatively successful, but not altogether happy, five years.

The hotel looked out to Capstan Hill and its flag pole and a wonderful sea view beyond. It had nine letting rooms arranged on three floors and could accommodate up to two dozen guests at any one time. It had its own car park and we inherited a number of loyal guests who came to stay year after year. It was very tastefully decorated throughout and was ideal for our ambition to offer holiday accommodation that was, literally, home from home. The lounge and bedrooms were decorated with various ornaments and our guests appreciated the ambiance. Twenty five years later we would still be in contact with some of the people who came as guests but departed as friends.

Initially I was on my own during the week as John was conscious of his duty to his examination classes and stayed to see out the rest of the school year at Backwell. He joined me every weekend and during the Easter holiday and, finally, full-time at the end of the summer term in mid July. By then, we could already see that we were not going to make our fortune from what turned out to be a very short summer season on the North Devon coast so John successfully applied for a teaching post at a comprehensive school in Barnstaple, some ten miles away. It meant going back down to the foot of the teaching ladder but, as our business bank loan came with an interest rate at an horrific eighteen percent, it seemed the sensible thing to do. After the summer season, John started at the Park School in the September.

We worked as an excellent team or double act: cleaning and tidying the rooms together after breakfast, me cooking and dishing up whilst John waited at table and both of us ignoring the dish washer whilst we made a game of trying to wash up by hand whilst staying ahead of the guests tackling their next course. Such games introduced a sense of fun into the more mundane jobs. Guests selected at breakfast from the evening menu which enabled me to offer a range of choices but anyone arriving new during the course of the day had to take 'pot luck'. Many a time new guests booked in just in time to eat the dinners we had put back for ourselves! I made all my own soups and bread rolls and the whole menu was home cooking to the best of my ability and, I like to think, much appreciated by all our guests. We only ever had one complaint – a fiery red-headed little man who arrived late with his wife and young child but who then objected to being offered a Hobson Choice Cottage Pie and left his portion with his fork sticking up vertically in the middle of it. John was so outraged at his rudeness that he suggested next morning that he (the guest) would, perhaps, be happier if he moved to another hotel. The rude little man said that he was content to stay but John then made it clear that he (John) would be happy on his behalf if he found alternative accommodation. 'Asterix' left!

I was booked by the local comprehensive school in Ilfracombe to do supply teaching during the winter months. The buildings are situated on the top the hill overlooking the town and up above The Georgian House. On many occasions, at the start and end of the season, when we had only a few guests, I could be seen sprinting up the hill behind the hotel with head down so as not to be recognised by departing guests who I had just finished serving at breakfast! Our naive dream of time-off and foreign holidays in the winter sun was never to materialise and we eventually realised that this kind of lifestyle was not for us. However, the past five years had given us a confidence (which we had previously lacked) in our ability to run a successful business. Our new venture, we decided, would be a Health Food shop based on a business in Ilfracombe High Street that we had perceived as doing rather well and where we thought we could gain specialist knowledge relatively easily

As one phase of our lives together closed we entered another, this time in Worle on the outskirts of Weston-super-Mare. In February 1986, we acquired an up-and-running café complete with staff which we planned to convert quickly into the health food shop. Why Weston? No particular reason and certainly not because it was John's home town. More a case of the right premises, at the right price, at the right time and in the right place.

Better, we decided, to start our own business from scratch in an area with a gap in the market than pay through the nose for someone else's success or, worst still, be saddled with their failure! Worle fitted the bill exactly and so on Valentine's Day we squeezed ourselves and three cats into a one-bedroom flat over the shop in Worle High Street. Suddenly, overnight, I was in charge of six staff and producing daily meals that were literally 'home cooked'. The frantic pace of this new life made the hotel seem like child's play in its simplicity but, with this move being a complete reversal of our previous one to Ilfracombe, John returned to his job in Barnstaple after the half term break and stayed in bed & breakfast accommodation Mondays to Fridays. Yet again I was left to cope on my own but this time felt that friends were close at hand and that I was less isolated.

As I grew to like the staff and became familiar with the café regulars, I began to get cold feet about closing what was obviously a successful and popular business. At Easter, the planned conversion to health food shop came and went undone. In September, John was able to get a term's fixed term contract at the local Churchill Comprehensive School which led, in turn, to a permanent post after the Christmas holiday and I was left with the day-to-day running of the business, the ordering and the complexities of the PAYE system. We still wanted to create the health food shop but, increasingly, wanted to retain the café. There clearly was not room for the two and we enquired about buying the ground floor shoe-repair shop next door with the idea of knocking through. The owner did not want to sell but we then came up with a more obvious solution – a single storey extension on our back garden which would be purpose built to accommodate the café whilst the original café was then converted into the Health Food shop. The two businesses would, hopefully, then serve to support each other since customers would have to pass through the shop to reach the cafe.

The new Coffee Garden café opened in the extension in May 1987 and was followed two weeks later by The Corn Dolly health food shop at the front. Now the hard work really started as I grappled to learn the intricacies of the supplements side of the business with the help of a new part-time member of staff, who had previously worked for Holland and Barrett.

By May 1991 we had saved sufficiently to buy our first real home together and were able to move out of the one-bedroom flat over the shop into a five-bedroom house built in 1917 at the southern end of Weston. This was literally the house of my dreams set in a large garden in a quiet part of the town and close to the seafront. I knew immediately on our first visit that this was the house I wanted: the warm atmosphere of a true family home enveloped us straight away adding, for my part, fuel to the increasing thoughts I had been entertaining of a family of our own. When we first married, John's previous vasectomy was a fact of life that I was happy to accept and one that I suppose, in the throes of an intense love affair, I had readily pushed to one side. As I reached thirty, friends and relatives who had previously been childless started producing families of their own and what had not been an issue in my twenties now became one in my thirties. John, I think, was aware of this even before I could admit it to myself and pushed me to discuss my feelings, something I have always been reluctant to do. His willingness to effect some answer to the situation was like a breath of fresh air and gave me a surge of hope. Many men in their late forties would not even have entertained the thought of starting a second family let alone have actively sought it. This, to me, was true commitment and the start of a journey that I would never have envisaged could be so long or so tortuous to achieve our dream.

The first positive step we took was to contact Social Services with a view to finding out about the adoption process. This seemed the most logical place to start and I can remember sitting in our flat over the shop having our first contact with a social worker. Far from being the positive step we had hoped for, it proved to be a thoroughly negative experience and dashed any hopes we might have entertained of adopting a baby. In the eyes of Social Services I was, at thirty four (and, clearly, John at fifty), already too old for this and the most we could expect would be to adopt an older child or one with special needs. Deflated, we felt this was not for us since I, like any first-time mum, was hoping for a baby. Our thoughts then turned to a biological child of our own and John went through a private reversal of his vasectomy in Bristol. With the original operation having been performed more than five years previously the chances of this succeeding were slim. Some sperm were produced but only a small number and a later second operation to remove a blockage had hardly better effect.

As our options began to dwindle and it appeared that John's ability to father a child was negligible, we both, perversely, became more determined to succeed! A new treatment, called Intra Cytoplasmic Sperm Injection (ICSI), was described on television where a single sperm could be injected into an egg but with this still in its infancy and only available in London, we did not follow it up. Through Southmead hospital in Bristol we were, after many tests, referred to St Michael's Hospital (also in Bristol) for artificial insemination by donor sperm which meant accepting that any child produced would be biologically half mine but bear no relationship to John. Although a disappointment it did not prove to be an insurmountable hurdle for either of us, just one more step along the journey.

This treatment turned out to be a major test of our commitment towards having a child. I defy any woman to remain sane whilst trying to predict her ovulation and act accordingly. This was done by means of a stick similar to a pregnancy testing kit (such a cruel analogy!) that looked for a particular hormone in the urine. With the optimum fertile period lasting only two days and failure to spot it meaning a wait of another month, testing was fraught. At £10 for a box of five sticks and the necessity to test twice daily it was vital to get it right. At the sight of the thin blue line an immediate dash to Bristol was required by us both leaving me free on the return journey to remain as invert as possible! Yes, we knew that gravity played no part in the proceedings but nothing was left to chance! Desperate measures for desperate people – and all this with no explanation to colleagues and staff who had to cover for us at the drop of a hat. The second visit on the following day at least gave the chance for a degree of planning, providing, of course, it was not a weekend when the clinic was closed!

We had both decided from an early stage that our attempts to be parents were for our knowledge only and it was better that family and friends thought us content as we were. This had the added advantage of a built-in let-out clause should we fail and no post mortems from concerned relatives, friends and colleagues.

A year later, with still no positive results, I was now classified as having 'unexplained infertility'. We plodded on, another step down the line and a referral to The Glen, a private BUPA hospital and reproduction clinic in Bristol. Around me friends, relatives and acquaintances all seemed to be expecting and salt was rubbed into the wound on a continual basis. If life had been difficult before it now became near impossible. Infertility brings its own stresses and tensions which, together with the invasiveness and stress of the treatment itself, leaves one to wonder how anyone can ever become pregnant in this manner.

There followed, in two short years, four treatments of IVF and one of GIFT, where unfertilised eggs and sperm are introduced, under general anaesthetic, into the fallopian tube via a small incision in the belly button. I, who had previously known nothing about fertility treatment, was fast becoming an expert at understanding the mechanics and the technical terms involved. I remember the anguish of the first treatment when my hopes were so high and I waited anxiously for the telephone call summoning me back to Bristol to have my fertilized eggs replaced in my womb. The call, when it came, reduced me to floods of tears as I listened to the news that not one had fertilized successfully and my chance of a pregnancy, together with another £2,000, had totally disappeared. How useless and stupid I felt, unable to do the one thing that comes so easily to so many.

But, reliving the nightmare was no help and the overwhelming desire to be pregnant made me pick up the pieces and carry on, convinced that this time I would become one of the statistics who were successful. That single, ultimate failure was never repeated and for the remaining three IVF treatments I had the luxury of knowing that three embryos had been replaced in my uterus. If that constituted pregnancy, then for those short and all too brief ten days I was well and truly pregnant. Ten long days of excuses to work colleagues spent resting in bed with only one thought on my mind. Days of praying and willing for an implantation with the clock ticking closer to the day when I might return to the clinic for the ultimate pregnancy test. A hope that was always dashed by the flow of blood heralding the start of my period, knowing that the eggs had died and my pregnancy with them.

Despite the setbacks, my resolve strengthened each time. After all, I could only win the lottery if I was a player! At the clinic I would meet with the other hopefuls although we rarely spoke but assessed each other silently comparing our chances. Was I younger, fitter, healthier and therefore more likely to become one of those golden statistics that the clinic was so proud to boast of? During my last treatment in May 1995 one girl in particular had become a close friend. Our cycles coincided, an unusual occurrence since I rarely saw the same couples twice. We met on two or three occasions, both with husbands with a failed marriage behind them and sharing a birthday at about the same sort of time. Vanessa was of a similar age and history to me and this alone gave us a link amongst the 'youngsters' with time on their side. We were able to draw strength from our failures and spoke several times on the phone. This was the only time that I was able to share my experiences and frustrations with anyone other than John and it was of enormous help. It was, however to be a last treatment for both of us since I moved on to achieve my ambition in a different way, whereas Vanessa was able to let go and became reconciled to a childless life.

From the autumn of 1994 we were increasingly aware that IVF might not be the success story that we had hoped for. It was now becoming harder to stimulate my ovaries to produce a significant number of eggs for collection since my hormone levels were rising. This indicated a pre-menopausal state with my chances of success decreasing. Our minds turned to foreign adoption as we witnessed in the media the plight of thousands of children in Third World countries. Surely we could offer a good home and love to such a child thus helping both them and us? John's visit to Michael Nicholson, the TV journalist and reporter, was based on such a news item from Sarajevo.

Again we made contact with Social Services to investigate their thoughts and policies on foreign adoption and waited weeks for the necessary social worker's visit to our home. They pointed out that we would need to identify a country and do most of the arranging ourselves, giving the impression that whilst not condoning foreign adoption they would do little to help either. The required home study could not be done by Avon County Council but would be passed on to a national agency with a time scale of about eighteen months and a cost of around £4,000. The final nail in the coffin for us was the knowledge that we could still be turned down with no refund after this was done and we would both be another year and a half older and still childless. Bearing in mind stories we had read in the media regarding other adoptions we felt that our combined ages and background would give 'them' every excuse to reject us. So, at that point, we decided to go it alone and make ourselves directly responsible for our own fate!

But, where to start? That was the question and not an easy one to answer. I wrote to the British Agency for Adoption and Fostering (BAAF) and received back some informative leaflets from which I learnt about designated and non-designated countries. The former were countries with which the UK had a reciprocal agreement, meaning that the courts here would recognise a foreign adoption as valid and the process would not need to be repeated once back in the UK. The adoption would be done with the full approval of Social Services and would require an authorised home study – the one hurdle we believed might trip us up. Having decided that that was not the route we wished to take, we were left with non-designated counties knowing that, having completed the adoption procedure in the child's country, we would have to apply to the British courts on our return for the making of a second adoption order in this country.

From the leaflets I identified about twenty such countries and wrote a standard letter to their London Embassies asking for details of their adoption process and requirements for adopters. These slowly returned with many varying conditions: for some we were too old, for others too young whilst a few countries appeared to have few rules and regulations whatsoever. From the Vietnamese Trade Delegation came a small compliments slip with the name of a Mrs Loveday handwritten on the bottom and a telephone number in London and, for us, that was where it all began!

6

Sue Loveday

John

The compliment slip said no more than *Dear Madam, please contact with Mrs Loveday at Tel… for adoption information of a Vietnamese child. Yours sincerely Mr Luc.*

We immediately assumed that Mrs Loveday worked for the Vietnamese Delegation and dealt with enquiries about adoption. I lost no time in writing to her – only to receive a somewhat guarded reply – headed by a Disclaimer stating that "whilst every effort has been made to ensure the accuracy of this factsheet, no claims can be accepted arising from errors". The fact sheet itself ran to ten foolscap pages of notes under various headings such as General Notes, Processing of Documents, Child Allocation, Visa Requirements, Formalities to be Completed, The Leaving Ceremony, Entering Britain and Re-adoption in the UK. It was wonderfully informative.

Sue Loveday, it turned out, was not some minor official working for the Delegation and answering questions about foreign adoption as we supposed but a single woman who, eighteen months previously, had adopted Jordan, then aged just eight weeks, from an orphanage in Hanoi with the help of a local woman. This was a turning point for us since it potentially gave us not only a direct link into Vietnam but, more importantly, the proof that what we were trying to do had been achieved successfully on a previous occasion and not too long ago. It was early 1995 and we made immediate arrangements to visit Mrs Loveday in North London.

Sue turned out to be a larger-than-life character who physically dominated a room with her size and personality. No one could have been more helpful or more concerned for us and it is directly attributable to her that we were eventually successful where many others have failed. Sue, as a single woman and looking after a semi-invalid mother had, by sheer guts and determination, achieved on her own what we were trying and hoping to do as a couple. Our spirits soared! Surely, for the two of us together, it would be so much easier?

Anne
We were bowled over by Joe, a lively, intelligent, handsome and happy child and very much at the centre of Sue's life. I could see also the close bond that existed between Joe and his grandmother who lived with them – never any question that Joe was anything other than Sue's natural child. I hoped that my child would bring as much joy to my own mother and experienced a growing sense of the 'rightness' of what we were attempting to do. Sue spoke of her time in Vietnam, the difficulties she had encountered and, more particularly, how she overcame them. Such information was to become invaluable to us later on.

Sue had been helped in her quest by a minor Vietnamese government official named Nguyen Chien with whom she had forged a close friendship. (In Vietnam, we were told, the family name comes before the given name. Women keep their maiden name on marriage whilst any children take their father's). It was Chien (usually referred to as Madam Chien) who had been able to steer Sue through the sea of paperwork and documents required by the Vietnamese, act as interpreter and smooth a path through the many vagaries of a convoluted system. Chien, we decided, was the key to the whole process and her potential involvement crucial to our success.

Sue

I had had a hysterectomy in 1990 and was unable to conceive but that did not prevent me from wanting a child and to be a mother. Unfortunately, being over thirty five years of age and unmarried, I was not considered suitable for a British adoption so I had no alternative but to look abroad. I obtained some information from a local nurse who had adopted from Peru and started to get involved with an organisation who befriended people who were interested in foreign adoption. They gave me a lot of tips about what to do but it still seemed like an impossible task.

I started to put together a dossier about myself which included financial, medical, psychiatric and personal information. This was then authenticated by a notary public.

I heard that it was easy to adopt from Thailand because the government there recognised the British Social Services and that you could go to that country on holiday and complete an adoption in two weeks! I arranged a holiday and flew to Bangkok with a lady friend. On the plane I told her that I wanted to get a baby – she was slightly shocked but excited!

We went to Bangkok and to the local Social Services where there was an enormous orphanage. However, I quickly learned that I would not be considered eligible to adopt in that country because of my unmarried status. As I left, one of the staff followed me outside and suggested that I should try neighbouring Vietnam. I straightaway contacted the Vietnamese Embassy in Bangkok and they faxed my dossier to Hanoi. My friend and I continued with our holiday whilst I awaited a reply but although I telephoned every day, none came. At the end of the holiday I advised Hanoi that, as I was so close, I intended to move on to that city but I was advised to return to London and await contact. The disappointment was huge.

Back in London I returned to my daily routine not really expecting to hear any more. Then, five months later and out-of-the-blue, an open envelope from Hanoi plopped onto my doormat. I was advised to go to the Vietnamese Consulate with my papers and a child would be located for me! I rushed to the Consulate and completed all the necessary paperwork... but still nothing happened and I decided to travel with my mother for a holiday in New Zealand.

However, at the end of that holiday and on a stopover in Sydney on our homeward journey, I received a message to telephone Vietnam. I spoke to a Mrs Chien in Hanoi who told me that 'a baby boy had been born and did I want him?'

I said yes, yes, yes! and wanted to go straight on to Hanoi there-and-then but was told to return to the UK and obtain the appropriate visa to enter Vietnam. My mother and I returned to London in a state of high elation and I set about putting together a host of baby paraphernalia to take with me. I also had to arrange suitable accommodation for my semi-invalid mother whilst I was away and chose an inexpensive nursing home in Dublin. It was to be an inspired choice!

After taking mother to Dublin I finally set out for Hanoi with an enormous case containing powdered milk, nappies and all the other items such as clothing I had been buying in preparation. When I first saw 'my' baby in an orphanage outside Hanoi he was eight weeks old and wrapped in rags. Many days later, back in the hotel room with the baby in one hand and a Johnson & Johnson baby book in the other I became an instant mother!

Eventually, my baby was issued with a passport and I obtained a visa for Thailand, our one stop on the way home. I did not, however, have the correct papers to get him into the UK so when we went to change flights in Bangkok we were not allowed to board. It was explained to me that any airline bringing passengers into the UK without the proper papers would be heavily fined! I was stranded in Thailand with a very young baby and had no alternative but to book into a local hotel.

Naturally, when I telephoned my mother, she was very distressed to hear my news and extremely worried about this turn of events. She confided in the matron who just happened to be an old friend of Dick Spring, a former foreign minister of the Irish Republic. A few days later this lady was able to seek his advice – only to be told that children under sixteen years of age did not require a visa to enter Eire. This was wonderful news since I was travelling to Eire to collect my mother in any event so, with the appropriate ticket for my baby, we were out of Bangkok on almost the next plane – but only after the closest scrutiny of my travel documents by airport officials.

On arrival at Heathrow I still had to go through immigration to get to the appropriate terminal for my onward flight to Shannon airport. I was asked if I was then continuing home to London and when I confirmed that I was I was given a six months temporary UK visa for the baby.

On our return to London I had quite a battle with the local Social Services and my son was made a ward of court.

49

It took me a further four years to re-adopt him through the British legal system – but, eventually, we were able to celebrate the successful conclusion of that lengthy process and I was able to obtain for my son a British passport.

I named him Jordan. Adopting him was the most rewarding experience of my life and changed me completely. Becoming a parent gave me the greatest joy and I have been truly blessed by the love we share.

Since then, I have adopted Ruby (born 16 September 1998) in Houston, Texas and Hazel (born 1 October 2000) in Alabama, Georgia both as newborn babies through adoption agencies in the United States of America. Now, in 2008, we all live on the Isle of Wight.

Anne
John and I promised Sue that we would keep in touch and went home to Weston-super-Mare where he telephoned Nguyen Chien the following day. It was Tuesday 4th April 1995.

7

Chien

John

I introduced myself to Chien and explained that I had obtained her details from Sue Loveday. She spoke warmly of Sue and asked after her – but was then adamant that she was unable to help us. I found her accent difficult to understand but gathered that she did not work in the appropriate government department anymore. I virtually pleaded with her; she was our only hope of achieving a child; if she could not help us, did she know of anyone else who might be able to do so?

I must have got through to her because she finally said that she would see what she could do and told me to telephone her again in September, in six month's time. I immediately wrote a reminder in the diary – as if either Anne or I would forget!

Anne knew of two Vietnamese brothers who attended Worle School where she frequently worked as a supply teacher. She was able to access the family's address from the school records and, following my conversation with Chien, I telephoned the parents to explain that we were hoping to visit Hanoi to adopt a young child and could we meet with them for any advice they might be able to give us? We were immediately invited to their home the following day, Wednesday 5th April.

Cuong (originally Chinese) and Huong Cao had escaped from Vietnam as boat people in the early 1980s and had eventually made their way to London with their small son. Another boy was born whilst they were held in a holding camp in the London area and eventually Cuong had found a job as a book-binder in Weston-super-Mare. They were both very interested in our hoped-for plans to visit Hanoi where Huong had still had relatives and Anne and I spent a very pleasant and interesting evening getting to know them and being given some very helpful advice about what life in that city was like. Cuong's command of English was better than Huong's, possibly because he was mixing more with English people in the workplace and he readily volunteered to translate any correspondence which arrived written in Vietnamese. Over the next few years we were to have a lot of help from Cuong in the two-way translation of letters and will be eternally grateful for his assistance.

After anxiously counting down the calendar over the ensuing months, I telephoned Chien again in September, as arranged. We were rather disappointed to find that she was still not in a position to help us but she asked me a few questions such as whether we wanted a boy or a girl, a baby or an older child and so on. I replied that we would prefer a baby, if possible, but either sex would be equally acceptable! She said that she would get back to me if and when a child became available. I assumed that this would be from an orphanage, as Jordan had been.

We waited.

8

Nov '95: The Preparations

Anne

The letter came totally out of the blue in late November telling us that, at last, Madame Chien was able to help us and listing the documents that we needed to send out to her. What incredible excitement this produced as, finally, it seemed that something was about to happen and we could take an active part instead of just passively sitting and waiting. We spent three weeks rushing around to get everything ready; the police reports indicating that neither of us had a criminal background, the medical examinations confirming that we were both in good health, various bank statements to convince the Vietnamese authorities that we were people 'of substance' and the necessary social worker's report. This last requirement would have proved a huge stumbling block had we not been able to benefit from Sue's experience and advice since, ploughing our own furrow so to speak, meant we had had, and were having, no further contact with Social Services.

Sue's own report had been done by Robin Carter, an independent social worker who lived in Newcastle. This was entirely acceptable to the Vietnamese and so John contacted him by telephone and a few days later Robin travelled down by train to Weston-super-Mare and spent a day interviewing us before going home to compile his report. Without the constant and implied criticism that we always seemed to associate with Social Services this was, by comparison, a relaxed and informal procedure. However, we both felt that Robin had done a good job and had been able, in that short time, to get a true measure of us, our feelings and our home circumstances. Finally, John took a day off work just a few days before Christmas and drove up to London to visit the Foreign and Commonwealth Office and then the Vietnamese Embassy to have all the documents ratified and stamped. These were then sent to Chien in Hanoi by the courier, DHL. There was nothing further we could do but sit and wait for her to contact us again.

At this stage, we had no idea if a specific baby had been assigned to us nor did we realise that there was any urgency in the situation. On Boxing Day, having already explained our plans to Mum a few days earlier, with all my family to lunch (Mum, my elder brother Brian and his wife, Anne, with their daughter, Michelle, and my older brother Ian with his wife, Marion, and their son, David) we 'exploded' our bombshell. The overwhelming reaction was of immense joy and Marion immediately burst into tears, overcome by the emotion of the situation. We had certainly covered our tracks well since no-one had realised that our childless state was anything other than by choice – which added to the enormity of our news. It was heart-warming to feel that everyone was behind us and boosted my confidence and courage which had ebbed and flowed like the tide.

Beforehand, making such an announcement had been

a huge worry for me since no longer could we hide behind the facade that our lives were as we wished them to be and the superstitious side of my nature had urged me not to tempt fate by telling anyone of our plans. However, there would be no other occasion when we would all be together in the near future and so it had to be now. The timescale was still an unknown factor and I realised afterwards that the family were all of the opinion that it would be a year or so before anything happened – making the speed of the events that followed even more amazing for them.

With Christmas out of the way we sat back and waited to hear from Chien. On Tuesday 2nd January, whilst we were still surrounded by Christmas decorations, Sue Loveday rang to say that Chien was frantic to speak with us. We could only assume that she had lost our telephone number but rang her the following lunchtime (early evening in Vietnam) and learned, for the first time, that a baby girl – a twin – was waiting for us and that we had to be in Vietnam as soon as possible!

At that moment an idea in the abstract became a baby in the reality and I felt physically sick at the enormity of what we were about to do. The news that the baby was a twin gave us great concern and we immediately assumed that they were being separately adopted. John told Chien that we would like to adopt both girls rather than see them separated but she told him that this was not possible. We were very distressed at the thought of the babies being parted and John told her that we did not want to be a party to their separation.

At that point, she then explained that the other twin was staying with the family. Apparently, the father had three older children from a previous marriage, two boys and a girl. His wife had left him with the children and he had subsequently remarried. His new wife had lost

55

her first baby through high blood pressure and had, quite unknowingly, fallen pregnant with twins on the second occasion. They were very poor rice farmers, living out 'in the sticks' some miles from Hanoi, and had not known that the woman was expecting twins until the first baby was born and the hospital medical staff announced that there was a second child waiting to be delivered. The parents subsequently decided to give up one of the twins for adoption in the belief that they could not afford to bring up five children to adulthood.

At that, our attitude completely changed and underwent a complete reversal. We just had to have this child because, at that very moment, we determined to do our utmost to keep the twins in touch with one another until such time in the future they would be able to take over that contact themselves. Maybe, one day, they could be together again. It was, by any stretch of the imagination, a desperately sad situation but we would do all we could, now and in the future, to keep the girls in touch with one another. If anyone else adopted the child being given up and she went to France, America or Sweden, she might never know that she had a family let alone a twin.

After ten years, it appeared that we were now at a crossroads in our lives and the countdown had begun!

9

Anne's Diary – Preparation

Thursday 4th January 1996
Today I bought my first baby clothes! A beautiful Christmas dress in black velvet and burgundy taffeta and also a navy blue velour sleep suit, both in the Boots sale. John has been in touch with two of our local travel agents to see how quickly he could arrange flights; more importantly, he has been in touch with the Vietnamese Embassy to enquire about visas. Apparently, these are for either business purposes or for tourism. Adoption, we decided, must come under tourism but such visas only cover a five-week period – and are non-extendable. Their issue, he was told, will take two weeks, possibly sooner if they rush it. John immediately sent off our applications, passports and the appropriate fee.

Friday 5th January
Help! Today I discovered that we're off in ten days time and real panic is starting to set in. Flights are booked for Tuesday 16th and the travel agents, Baker Dolphin, have proved extremely helpful. How on earth can I be ready in time – are we mad?

Used the *Admag*, the local freebie, and bought some second hand baby clothes from a young woman in Bridge Road and also a few other bits and pieces such as a bottle heater – ostensibly for my expectant daughter! Oh, the irony of the situation! Got in touch with Karen Harris, a neighbour who lives opposite, who was a big help – once she had picked herself off the floor! Said she would jot down a list of what I might need since I really didn't have a clue and she has two young children of her own.

My first afternoon back in school after Christmas, so had to explain to my Head of Department, Maggie Heath, that I would be taking time off and would be unable to supply cover for the school ski trip (22nd – 26th Jan) for which I had been pre-booked. Shame, as such a big chunk of money would have been useful.

Saturday 6th January

Sue and Joe came for the weekend at short notice. Very supportive as always and gave me some last minute advice. Really helpful to understand exactly what shortages we will experience when we get there and exactly what items we should take both for us and the baby. We're still very concerned about our entry back into the UK since the baby will have no visa as we have not followed the 'system'. Robin Carter's unofficial home study, whilst acceptable to the Vietnamese, would certainly make problems were we to attempt to apply for visa for the baby at this stage and is not something we feel like putting to the test. Consequently, we're following the Ireland route as advised by Sue and have tickets returning Hanoi – Heathrow – Dublin as the Irish don't require visas for children under sixteen. If Heathrow won't let us in we'll fly on to Dublin and return via Bristol International Airport or by ferry hoping that a return from an EEC country will mean that no customs are involved. Sounds fine in theory but still a huge worry and a bridge we'll cross when we come to it.

Sunday 7th January

Invited Gill and Rod (John's sister and her partner) round for coffee mid morning to meet Sue and to pass on our news which we still haven't told them. Unfortunately, Gill unwell so only Rod came – itching to know what was going on as John had sounded so intriguing on the phone! I've never seen anyone so totally pole-axed but so happy for us and he couldn't wait to rush off to tell Gill who he knew would be absolutely delighted, too. This she confirmed when she rang later, owning that the only really serious news they could think off was a divorce announcement! Oh, ye of little faith!

Monday 8th January

Back to work and shop open after a long Christmas break. Time now to tell the 'girls', Mandy and Jan today who were both over the moon. No time to back out now. This is REAL!

Tuesday 9th January

Gwyneth at work today and I felt a little concerned at telling her since it's not that long since she lost her own daughter who had died whilst au pairing in Canada. She was weepy but, again, very happy for us, as is everyone. Another bombshell at 1pm – John had heard from Mme Chien and would we like to adopt a baby boy as well? Thirty seconds to decide. What the hell! YES! It can't be any harder than what we're doing already. When she rang back for an answer, John tried to find out the size of either baby. She thought the girl was about 4 ½ kgs. (This turned out to be completely wrong and was the cause of everything I took being far too big.)

59

Visited doctor's late afternoon for a battery of jabs which made both arms really hurt. Really too close to departure so it may be that we're not covered initially during our first week out there but nothing else we can do.

Wednesday 10th January
Both arms still very sore and I got little sleep last night – too much worry! Today I feel really panicky – a constant sick feeling in my stomach. What are we doing? Back to Boots again and another £50 spent on items for baby no 2. This one is 18 months old so probably on solids. What to buy is a real problem. I've still got nothing to carry either of them in and this is causing me great concern and I feel rather weepy. I must calm down. The jabs might well be having some effect, too.

Thursday 11th January
In school all day as a supply teacher. Some rotten classes but might as well earn money whilst I still can! Still loads of shopping to do; it's unbelievable how much I have to get, not just for the babies but also because of the climate. Bought a Miriam Stoppard baby book which will be an instant guide to being a mum and will have to substitute for the umpteen antenatal classes I would otherwise have had if I'd be about to give birth – how to change a nappy for a start! All sorts of arrangements are being made daily, especially to do with the shop. I've made out a weekly job rota which falls especially heavily on Mandy and have asked them to repeat it until we return, hopefully in 2-2 ½ weeks time. Large suppliers have been asked to hold bills until we return, whilst smaller ones can be paid out of the till. Everyone has been allocated a given day to take their wages out of the till and every other day Rod will come over to collect the takings to put into envelopes John has

prepared for the purpose. Gill will then keep them at home until our return. That seems to cover most everyday occurrences; let's hope nothing out of the ordinary happens!

John has arranged for a young friend, Mark Gillespie, to house-sit whilst we're away, a brilliant idea which solves the problem of leaving the cats and the house in winter. Mark arrived this evening for a meal and to go over final details. With both the house and shop sorted I feel able to concentrate finally on the journey itself. Katrina, Jan's daughter, has been really helpful and has been able to borrow loads of baby clothes for me to save buying. All the time I've been very cagey about telling people our plans as I feel it might be somehow possible for Social Services to put a halt to what we are planning. Katrina gave all sorts of ridiculous reasons to friends as to why the clothes were needed but, in the end, had to come clean!

Friday 12th January

The passports are back but we are rather concerned to note that the visas are only valid for five weeks from 9th January so we will have wasted a week before we fly out. They will expire on 12th February and are non-extendable. Too late to do anything about it now but since we believe that we will only be away for about three weeks, hopefully there won't be a problem. Managed to fit in a hair cut with Lynn, my regular hairdresser for many years and one more person now told. Into town for more shopping, this time two tiny silver bracelets, one for each twin as a symbol linking them together. Finally managed to buy a second hand carrying papoose and have decided to use two slings for travel which will keep both hands free. I'll worry about sleeping arrangements when we arrive. My last afternoon in school before we leave. My last time as a DINKY (double income, no kids yet!). Exam invigilation is an easy option that I'm more than happy to undertake.

I'm finally starting to feel more organised now and can actually believe that we will be leaving the country on Tuesday and it is not just a fairy tale! Had a worrying phone call from David Revell this evening (he and his wife had also adopted in Vietnam and had been helped by Chien. We had been introduced to them by Sue Loveday) and he wanted to tell us about the problems they were now having with their adoption. Did we realise how difficult it might be? Neither of us could understand why he had rung at this late stage and it most definitely was not what we wanted to hear. John became very shirty with him and literally told him to 'bugger off' and I ended up feeling rather depressed. Anyway, we'll worry about those problems after we return. One step at a time!

Saturday 13th January
Both manning the shop today, as usual on a Saturday – John's last time before we leave. In the afternoon I did some last bits of shopping and bought a silver St Christopher for the baby boy. Also some local postcards of Weston-super-Mare scenes to show the family and Chien. Our last weekend as a childless couple!

Sunday 14th January
Gill and Rod came round for coffee and for a final chat. We had booked to meet old friends from Ilfracombe at a local carvery but they were unable to make it and sent us their best wishes explaining that our latest scheme confirmed their suspicion that we must be mad! We went alone, a kind of 'last supper' for the two of us. Sue Loveday rang in the evening to wish us well and we spent time doing some packing. John had had the superb idea of taking two large polystyrene boxes into which we managed to pack all the

baby milk, food and nappies. This made a huge difference and left the cases free for clothes – baby not ours – having limited ourselves to virtually nothing! A light-hearted film rounded off the evening leaving little time to think or worry.

Monday 15th January
Feel really sick and nervous today, do we really want to do this? After all, life will never be the same again and how can we possibly cope with the shop and all we're used to doing? Still, can't back out now, I would never forgive myself as it definitely is what we both want and this chance is never going to occur again. Giving birth has got to be a cinch compared to all the turmoil we're going through.

Last day at work for both of us. John has negotiated three weeks leave, with both the partners at his firm thinking he must be totally nuts, especially as he's only in the first few months of his two-year training contract – previously known as articles. Managed to keep busy and tried not to think too much; some more shopping and managed to get a white hooded baby suit aged three months which will be great for travelling and, hopefully, okay size-wise. Goodness knows what I've spent in the last ten days but I guess it's still only a fraction of what a normal layette would cost. Had a lovely card from Jan and the girls in the shop, still can't believe we're just upping and leaving them to it. Spoke to all the family that evening with all their love and good wishes passed on. John went to play in a skittles match with the rest of his team leaving me to fiddle around with various last minute jobs. Finally, bed at 11.15pm and actually a good night's sleep, probably from emotional exhaustion knowing there was nothing else we can possibly do.

10

Into The Unknown

Tuesday 16th January

This day should be carved on our hearts forever along with many of the others that will follow. For ordinary, everyday people it really does feel as though we are doing something so incredibly brave and pioneering. I woke up feeling full of nerves with a sick feeling in the pit of my stomach. It was cold and wet when we got up at 5.45am but we had little that needed to be done before Rod arrived at 6.45am. Gill had decided not to come as space in the car is needed for luggage. We have a large suitcase for the babies and a medium-sized one for us plus the two blue boxes and two pieces of hand luggage. A quick goodbye to the cats who knew something was up and we were off.

A long delay at junction 10/9/8 on the M4 due to road works and an accident left us starting to panic. Finally arrived at 9.20am – less than two hours to departure. An emotional goodbye to Rod and with our luggage checked in with no problems we went through to the departure lounge. John purchased a bottle of gin to keep in our hotel room and after an added delay of an hour and a half due to fog we finally boarded. I couldn't believe that this was really it and we were truly on our way. The thirteen hour flight seemed to take forever but at least the delay at Heathrow had reduced our waiting time in Singapore from four hours to two. Changi airport was fantastic and a real revelation after Heathrow with so much to see and do. It was now early morning and it was odd not to have been to bed. We put our watches on eight hours on landing. Another forty-five minutes delay due to engine problems and eventually our smaller Vietnamese plane takes off. It was a good flight but the nearer we got to Hanoi the more nervous I became. Before, our travelling had found us in a kind of limbo but as we neared our final destination we were constantly reminded of our purpose by the sea of Vietnamese faces that surrounded us on this leg of the journey. Vietnam had only been opened up to tourists about six years ago and Europeans were still very few and far between!

Wednesday 17th January

This day never really had a starting point since, not having gone to bed, two days merged into one. We flew over Laos and the intestinal loops of the river in the Mekong Delta, straining to catch a glimpse out of the window of the ground below us. The views were spectacular with good visibility and bright sunshine and we followed the verdant green spine of Vietnam as the plane droned northward.

As we neared our destination we could see the countryside unfolding below us – very green and frequently divided into mile after mile of paddy fields. We also spotted what looked like small cemeteries amongst the paddy fields studded with gravestones, some quite elaborate, that suggested that people are sometimes buried on their own land. As we flew lower we could make out men and women working in the fields up to their calves in water.

Here and there men seemed to be pushing old-fashion ploughs through the water and we saw one pulled by an ox. Everything looked very primitive and was all the more interesting for that. The scenery brought home the fact that we were about to enter a completely different world.

In a comparatively short while we were coming into land at Noi Bai airport and could see coolie-hatted farmers working paddy fields which, to our surprise, came right up the edge of the runway. Our descent showed us just how different this country would prove to be. Along the side of the runways were many locals, pushing bicycles and even farming, wearing loose clothes and large coolie hats, the 'uniform' of the Vietnamese peasant. Such a contrast to England, where this would be a prohibited area.

By the time we landed I was feeling absolutely petrified. To come all this way, both physically as well as emotionally, what were we doing? Suppose I took one look at the baby and didn't like, let alone love her? After all, some natural mothers don't bond with their children after conceiving them and nurturing them for nine months. Here we were, contemplating a baby or even babies from another world and another culture. How could maternal love possibly kick in?

At this stage I was in such a panic that I had fully decided not to go ahead if I felt at all unhappy about the situation. But what a turmoil and mix of emotions I had to cope with; all the money we had spent which we couldn't possibly afford to spend again; it really did have to be now or never!

It was 2.20pm local time, the equivalent of 8.20pm British time. Strangely enough, Vietnam is only seven hours ahead of the UK so our watches went back one hour on this flight from Singapore. After travelling for twenty-five hours, we were exhausted.

As soon as we disembarked we could feel the heat and humidity envelop us like an oppressive shroud. I, who had never experienced the like before, could immediately understand and give sense to things previously read about such a climate, so alien to our world. Ahead, a collection of low level corrugated iron huts marked the airport terminus – at least half a century behind the times. Soldiers everywhere and, of course, with guns – so intimidating for us not used to a military presence. Queues and checks for everything, much form filling, usually in triplicate and always under the watchful eye of the militia.

I feel like a criminal before we've even begun!

Eventually, we were able to pass through the arrival area and were met by the taxi driver Chien had promised, another minor worry surmounted! And what a journey the ride into Hanoi proved to be! It was as though we had travelled back many decades as we watched the picture unfolding on either side of the car. The fields were being worked by peasants in the traditional uniform as described earlier with either open-toed sandals or bare feet. Only a few cows visible and of obvious value as each was tended by a single person, usually a child. As for the traffic on the road itself, well that description defies belief – we travelled on a fairly new and wide tarmacadamed highway where the Keep Right rule seemed to apply only loosely. Tooting at all and sundry seemed to be the order of the day and most people adopted a centre line approach, swerving at the last minute if something was in the way. Amazingly, we remained unscathed despite, to my mind, many near misses. Eventually, the flatness of the fields gave way to a more urban appearance as we entered the outskirts of Hanoi and began passing continuous rows of small narrow shops rather like open garages with people sitting around outside each of them. It is such an alien scene for both of us and all the more fascinating for that. The drive from the airport has taken about forty five minutes and we eventually turned one last corner and drew up outside a small hotel. It was 3.45pm and we had arrived at the Dream 2 Hotel, as recommended by Chien and booked from England.

A 'special' room had been put aside for us as we were, apparently, to be there for 'a month'! Not the news we were expecting to hear but we will argue about that later. The air-conditioning in our room is good, the room itself small and rather gloomy but adequate. In one corner a fridge, a very up-to-date TV with satellite, a large comfortable bed, a small wardrobe and a desk, two armchairs and an adjoining bathroom with bath and overhead shower and a flush toilet. None was finished to a high standard but, as we were to realise later, this was sheer luxury compared to what most people in Vietnam had.

John leaves me to unpacked whilst he switches on the television set to see what sort of programmes might be available for our entertainment. As the picture flickers into focus, to our utter amazement it shows a European audience with Mike Roe, one of John's fellow members of our local Conservative Association in Weston, apparently asking a question of a panel of speakers. As John fumbles to increase the volume it becomes clear that he has accessed Question Time from Bristol on the BBC's World Service. How bizarre that we should have travelled nearly half way round the world only to see someone who lives barely a mile away from us at home! The camera then panned to another member of the audience who has been a regular customer at The Corn Dolly! What odds would we get on such a coincidence?

We decided to go for an exploratory walk. What an experience that proved to be! On most roads into the centre of Hanoi the traffic was almost 'wall-to-wall' – mainly bikes and mopeds whose riders beep and toot continuously at the rider in front who, in turn, ignores the vehicle behind whilst signalling the one in front. It was a cacophony of noise that assaulted the eardrums non-stop. Crossing the road seemed to be a suicidal mission since there appeared to be no break in the traffic – until we discovered the local method which we quickly adopted: fix your eyes on a point on the other side of the road, step out (bravely!) into the traffic and walk at a slow, constant speed to that point looking neither left nor right as you do so or you will most likely lose your nerve! Believe it or not, everything then swerves around you until you have gained the sanctuary of the other side. The parting of the Red Sea came to mind!

Everything had to be seen to be believed; open drains, (not sewers, we decided) in which the vegetables for the many small cafes were washed, food being cooked on the pavements on small burners then sold to anyone who cared to stop and eat, men squatting playing cards, everybody busy doing – not much, it seemed.

As we approached the lake at the city's centre we were intercepted by a young girl around twelve years of age selling postcards but we politely but firmly declined having decided to wait until we had a better knowledge of the city before making such purchases. However, this vivacious child spoke quite good English and was particularly persistent – proceeding to tell us that both her father and mother were dead so would we buy her postcards? We commiserated with her but politely declined and moved on. Later, we were approached by small groups of other children – girls selling postcards and shoeshine boys who appeared to be even younger. We were also accosted by beggars, many of whom were handicapped in some way.

As 'foreigners' we seemed to be a rare curiosity and a target for all of them.

On our return an hour later we were given the message that Chien would meet to eat with us at 7.30pm. I was again very nervous as I felt that it was important to make a good impression and develop a rapport with her since she would be crucial to our plans. When she arrived she turned out to be a small, slight, elegantly dressed woman with black, short, very curly hair and aged about forty. She appeared business-like and efficient with a friendly smile that I somehow never felt quite sure about. My impression of her in the flesh was only marginally better than on the phone, which would prove to give us huge problems in the future. We spent the evening chatting to her, showing her a range of postcards giving views of Weston-super-Mare and photographs of our home and presented her with gifts of chocolates and a silver brooch made from Welsh silver. We had discussed this small act beforehand in detail not sure of the protocol involved with presents.

We tried to impress on her that we had not much more than a two-week deadline to complete the adoption without, we hoped, appearing to put pressure on her. Our tourist visas were only valid for a five-week period and, unfortunately, almost one week had already expired before we left the UK. Her explanation of the procedure was, at times, lost with our limited ear for her accent.

(On comparing notes afterwards we would invariably discover that we both had a different understanding of what she had said. We would learn in the future to question and repeat everything until it was clear in our minds but even this did not always work.)

Staying at the same hotel is a French couple, Antoine and Jacqueline Saavedra, who were also in Vietnam to adopt. They are here with the full blessing of their

Government although they are independently finding their own child. Somehow, their paths had crossed with Chien and she had recommended the Dream 2 Hotel to them – reinforcing our suspicion that Chien was, perhaps, on a commission. They were a pleasant couple and since Jacqueline's English mother had married a Frenchman she had relatives in the Midlands and spoke very good English. They were interested to ask about our visa and how it was possible to adopt two children at the same time. We felt very uneasy discussing such things and answered somewhat evasively. By the end of the evening, however, I was convinced that to attempt to adopt two children would be more than a bridge too far and we explained this to Chien before she left having arranged that we would see the baby girl tomorrow. We spent a sleepless night, despite our tiredness, worrying about what the next day would bring.

Thursday 18th January

We were up at 9am and had the morning free until we were due to meet Chien at 1.30pm. Breakfast was fine: coffee, omelette, bread and jam. The International Bank is on the other side of the city, a good stretch by foot and, once there, we spent an hour trying to sort out a withdrawal with only a limited amount of English being spoken. In the end we had to take out all our money and transfer it to a savings account so we could access it as we needed. There was a small number of what appeared to be Europeans being served or waiting but we did not hear English being spoken. The bank staff, although very helpful, all looked so young. It must be an Asian thing.

We went back to the hotel. Chien arrived at 1pm but the taxi bringing the baby and her mother from the village did not turn up until 2.35pm. Passed an incredibly anxious time waiting not knowing what to think or feel, all the time in the hotel foyer trying to make small talk. Acceptance of a cup of tea from the hotel staff produced a tiny cup of the most evil brew it has ever been my misfortune to taste – a variation, I suspect, on green tea but definitely not something either of our palates could easily take to.

At last the taxi arrived and we stood to greet a very petite woman carrying a tiny bundle totally invisible under a large (for her) blanket – which I later realised was half a cotton floor mat. She had an attractive but very tired-looking face and long black hair pulled back tightly into a ponytail. She smiled at us shyly but, of course, we couldn't communicate directly. Her hands were small and appeared rather dirty with the nails cut short and square, the tips black – hands that looked used to hard manual work. She was simply dressed in cotton trousers, a blouse, an anorak and with plastic 'jellies' on her feet. Chien introduced her as Ghi – pronounced as 'gee' with a hard g.

She sat on one of the chairs in the lobby tightly clutching the baby and John and I were both unable to check the tears as we gazed down on this little scrap who looked so small, helpless and beautiful – a tiny face and wearing more than one hat. The emotion overcame us both as we realised that in front of us was the very reason that we had travelled half way round the world. And yet, through our joy, we could not help but feel so desperately sad for this woman who is having to give up this child. Our joy is her pain and the doubts threaten to crowd in and overwhelm us.

The moment was broken by the practicalities we faced. We were to take the baby to the Swedish Medical Centre for a medical examination. Only room for four in the taxi (including the driver) and, to my horror, John was told by Chien that he would have to stay behind. I felt very vulnerably and abandoned. I sat next to the mother and baby in the back of the taxi conscious of their different smells – a world away from what I was used to. We arrived in a short space of time at a very clean modern-looking building and I was enormously relieved to find that English was spoken. My confidence reappeared when faced with a situation that I recognised. I was ushered into another room with the baby which Ghi had carefully handed to me. The first time of holding. It seemed so strange. Could this tiny scrap ever really be my baby?

I was told to undress her on a flat table and struggled to divest her of layers and never-ending layers of clothes; four T-shirts carrying various motifs all in English, three hats (one made from a handkerchief), a 'neck rag' (presumably to mop up milk), a pair of bright pink socks and a triangular piece of thin cotton material tied round her lower body to form a 'nappy'. It seemed appropriate to put on a nappy from the bag that I had brought with me, a first for her. She was none too clean and the clothes were filthy, the smell so alien to me. The scales showed her to be 2.74 kg – 6lbs – at three months, only equivalent to a small newborn in England!

Finally, after many tests by Dr Kot Rafi and his immediate staff, all the results were given as negative except for syphilis which won't be available for a few days. The relief was palpable, another hurdle passed. A sudden smell and the nappy needed changing already. With no book to use, would I pass the first test? The faeces were yellow, loose and very evil smelling. It was a baptism of fire without any shadow of a doubt. The Swedish doctor was excellent: a low iron count was diagnosed and a multivitamin prescribed with a dropper. I parted with $172 US dollars and was given a phone number to ring for the results on Sunday. I rejoined the others and handed the baby back to her mother. In the taxi I gave Chien 300 dollars for expenses to come, handed over small presents of chocolates and soap to Ghi. Separate beings linked only by the baby. I was dropped back at the hotel and they left without seeing John again. I recounted the events. An excellent meal was served at 7pm; fish in a lemon sauce with rice followed by mixed fruit. Bed early at 10.30pm but it was 3.30am before I slept, the events of the day crowding around inside my head.

11

Waiting…

Friday 19th January

The alarm went off at 7am but 7.45am before we arose, both so very tired. An early breakfast, even managed to get some fried eggs today. It's much colder, thank goodness! Visited the Bank again, no problems with withdrawals; located the British Embassy for future reference and wandered round the city. The arrangement of shops was fascinating. Every street given over to its own trade – very much like Butchers Row in Barnstaple where a small road is occupied by nothing other than butchers' shops. Here, a road given over to the manufacture, repair and sale of shoes. Turn a corner and everyone was making, engraving and selling gravestones. Turn another corner – watches and clocks. Another and it was clothes and so it went on. In more prominent streets we found garments made of silk, probably for the tourist trade. Further out we later found decorated flower and plant pots and, on the outskirts, blacksmiths creating wrought iron work on the pavements outside their units. But nowhere did we see a mixture of outlets and surmised that the system ensured that there is no competition between adjacent businesses with regard to prices.

Although the streets and many of the buildings seemed to be filthy, the people themselves looked very clean and we marvelled how they could achieve such white blouses and shirts when, presumably, everything was hand-washed and, from what we could see, in cold water. However, everyone either wore plastic 'jelly' shoes that we only knew as beachwear at home or went bare-footed. People sat around in the doorway of their tiny shop units or squatted on the pavement outside patiently waiting for someone to come along who might like to buy something. In the city centre, near the lake, a small group of female money-changers lurked near the Post Office and there was even a couple of women close by each with a simple set of bathroom scales hoping that someone would come along who wanted to be weighed for the cost of a pitifully small amount of dong, the Vietnamese currency.

It seemed impossible to believe that we were really here. We watched rubbish being collected by women with brooms and hand carts. One found a dead rat and held it up by the tail. Later we were to see a group of women preparing flowerbeds. I don't think that we ever saw men doing this type of manual work.

The indoor market is unbelievable; smells and sights so foreign to us. Dead dogs were stretched out both with and without heads, some raw, some cooked. Fish flapped in small bowls, no hygiene regulations here! Then, suddenly, we bumped into Chien pushing her bicycle whilst shopping, a vast coincidence in a city of some three million people. We walked with her to some offices to collect the adoption papers and had to obtain three photocopies from a local shop. We took a cyclo to return to the hotel, a tricycle ridden by a local man with a carriage attached to the front, just enough room for two passengers but still a bit of a squeeze for two Europeans. We have spent every day since our arrival feeling like two Gullivers in the land of the Lilliputians and this ride merely served to reinforce that feeling as the cyclist strained at the pedals even though the entire journey was on the flat. The ride was not for those of a nervous disposition given the denseness of the traffic and, as usual, every road-user's total disregard for other vehicles – especially as we were both at the sharp end of this one!

Chien, on her bicycle, met us at the hotel and stayed with us to help complete the adoption forms in triplicate and explain the whole adoption procedure to us. It would be impossible for us to leave before 3rd February so flights must be changed and money could now be a problem since we had bargained for a stay of around three weeks only. Our anxieties levels increased!

After she left at 1.30pm we slept until 6pm as we were so tired. A good meal again and spoke to the French couple who, it seems, are planning to be in Hanoi for six weeks whilst they adopt. This is not what we want to hear! A walk seemed a good idea, it might help us sleep later and we visited the Old Quarter, becoming lost and eventually finding Ho Chi Min's Mausoleum. Large amounts of money have clearly been spent here! Back at the hotel we treated ourselves to the luxury of a gin and tonic from our supplies.

Saturday 20th January
Up late and breakfasted at 10am. A poor night for John who was awake from 3.50am. The French couple are worried as there seems a possibility that their baby might have Hepatitis B. They cannot understand how our test could have been done so quickly when theirs has taken days. In a huge panic I tried to ring Dr Rafi to make sure our test was authentic. Line engaged so the problem not solved.

We walked to the Singapore Airline office where flights were changed (the first of many visits) and bookings made for both the 3rd and 5th February to hedge our bets, so to speak. We walked to the market and stood for ages on a street corner just watching the traffic negotiate the junction, sheer magic that all survived with no accidents. We both feel rather uncomfortable at the thought of another two weeks here since we are so restricted in where we can go. We would love to travel outside the city but dare not because we don't know what is due to happen next or, more to the point, when it will happen. We just can't risk being away from the hotel next time Chien suddenly wants us for the next step in the process. No simple holiday this. So much at stake that we are lifted beyond the role of tourists into a place where we feel neither fish nor fowl, separated from all around us and everything totally beyond our control.

It would be an interesting relief to venture out of the city and visit some of the wonderfully fascinating places beyond Hanoi but the adoption timescale is a constant mystery to us and we do not dare to venture far. Back to the hotel by cyclo, the poor driver took a wrong turning so had really earned his money by the time we got there. To be driven in such a way seemed somehow wrong but it at least affords the drivers a living. Back at the hotel the French couple had been to see Dr Rafi with 'their' baby borrowed from the orphanage for the occasion and he had done a new instant test, the same as ours, which he claimed was 99.9% reliable. This proved negative for them and they were having a repeat done to be certain. They were much happier now and so were we! They have already spent two weeks here and it could be wasted time. As Jacqueline is an immunologist she knows quite a bit about these things.

Spent five minutes chatting to the receptionist, Anh, on our way out. She is probably in her early 20s and is very friendly and pleasant. A busy life for her: seven days a week 7am – 2pm at the hotel then six days a week at University 5.30pm – 8.30pm and, on four days, Computer Studies from 3-5pm. All school and other studies must be paid for and no-one seems afraid of hard work.

Wherever we go we seem to attract attention from beggars and people selling things on the street. I feel like a walking dollar on legs and give some Vietnamese dong to some of the beggars. Goodness knows how they can live when all medical care must be paid for and there's little state aid to live on. It is, to us, such a place of contrasts: TVs and motorbikes side by side with people cooking and virtually living in the street. Everywhere we go we see rubbish piled up, brushed from within the houses and shops and left lying around outside. Again, it's women who tour the streets with their hand carts sweeping up and collecting the rubbish with their faces covered by a mask. Very few Europeans to be seen; mostly French with some Americans in evidence from time to time. We are constantly attracting stares from local people but this is only curiosity and at no time do we ever feel threatened or uncomfortable. We smile a lot and try to appear friendly.

Back at the hotel we make a pot of tea and have a short rest. We find the tea here most peculiar, quite strong and no milk anywhere to be found except powdered or condensed. Our morning coffee contained so much condensed milk that it was almost possible to stand up a spoon in it!

The buildings themselves are most unusual in that they are very tall and narrow and apparently very expensive by Vietnamese standards. They are only one room wide and most seem to have a motorbike ramp at the front, even into shops. Rebuilding seems to take place occasionally by pulling one building down between two others and slowly replacing it using wooden props and scaffolding. The few modern hotels that we see have mainly been squeezed between older buildings in stark contrast to them.

An old film, The Virgin Queen starring Bette Davis, was on TV and provided a little light relief from the hurly burly of the outside world. Afterwards, we went out to locate Cuong and Huong Cao's relatives who live in Van Mieu, a street not too far from the hotel. We easily found their small chemist shop and introduced ourselves. Not an easy task since they only spoke Vietnamese and a little French. A telephone number was dialled and we spoke to a cousin who arranged to meet us tomorrow at 9am though for what, we were not quite sure! We wandered round an area where many embassies were situated, not far from the Temple of Literature, Vietnam's oldest university. The Russian Embassy was quite magnificent showing their close involvement with the country and its communist links. Outside we saw women laying small paving bricks in a sand base. They were dressed in old clothes and wore coolie hats and sandals. As usual, the work was being undertaken in a very labour-intensive way and we were fascinated by scenes that we would never see repeated in the West. Again, we observed that it was most often women who were tackling manual work of this kind.

We crossed our busiest road yet; eyes fixed on the other side and a constantly maintained speed saw us safely over. This was one thing we felt we had mastered! We passed the railway line which passed quite close to our hotel. We can regularly hear the trains from our room. As it was the main line between North and South Vietnam we fully expected it to be fenced off from all around but, to our amazement, nothing could have been further from the truth! The line crossed several roads with pedestrian protected from machine by just a hand-operated, pull-across barrier in some places – quite unsophisticated for near city centre locations. It was possible to take a short cut to the next road along the railway line past people squatting at the side of the track sorting plastic bottles and cardboard. The doors of houses and small shacks opened within a few feet of the side of the track. Little Health and Safety control here!

Despite getting lost only a short distance from the hotel we eventually returned to our evening meal of fish in a meat sauce. Lots of bones included and John ate very little. The increasing stress of the situation and the lack of variety in the food we are eating is starting to depress him. We had arranged to visit The Puppet Theatre in the evening with the French couple and Chien. It was not an expense we really wanted to incur but it seemed churlish to refuse. We were escorted from the hotel by the male receptionist who obviously thought it cold since he wore a Russian fur hat! It was an interesting and very clever show and, to our amazement, there was a large number of Europeans there some having arrived by coach on the first organised tours we had seen. We returned by cyclo and had our first good laugh for ages as we organised a race between France and England, even overtaking mopeds on the way! We all had a drink from the hotel bar together with Chien whose bike had been stolen and who was riding her daughter's. We all enjoyed some more jokes that seemed to act as a kind of bonding session and helped to improve our relationship with her.

After she left we stayed chatting to Jacqueline and Antoine about the problems of understanding, payments and so on – which proved to be most interesting for us. They had had the result of the further test from Dr Rafi which was also negative and so they were very pleased. They had also spent some time talking to him and Jacqueline, professionally, thought him very competent. This in turn, made us feel much happier and more relaxed since we still had some doubts as to the validity of the test results we had been given.

11.15pm
Scotland v England rugby live on TV. John's cup has surely run over!

Sunday 21st January
Up early as we had to be at Van Mieu at 9am. John was again awake for two hours in the night although I slept reasonably well. No niece at the chemist shop so the family rang her and we spoke on the phone. Offers of help if we needed it to locate a baby but we assured her that all seemed okay and she was pleased. We were invited through to the back of the shop to have a hot chocolate drink and could see first hand the living conditions which, we assumed, were typical of the city. In one corner was an old shower where the dishes were washed in cold water and there were little signs of cleanliness or comfort anywhere. It was all very dismal, dark and depressing, no comparison to the conditions of comforts we would expect in England. We were made to feel very welcome, were shown photos of the Caos and were given two calendars, one for us and one to pass on to their relatives when we returned to Weston.

We left to walk to the lake in search of an English newspaper. Some sort of link with the 'real' world would have been very comforting but no luck and the British Embassy, where we might have been able to gain advice, was closed until Monday. Everywhere we passed seemed to show signs of decay; it was impossible to tell whether buildings were going up or being pulled down. Around the lake, shoeshine boys and postcard sellers were incredibly persistent. Beggars seemed to be able to home in on us from miles away.

Then, suddenly, there was the young girl with her postcards who we'd seen on our first walk to the lake. She homed in on us without any sign of recognition (do we all look alike?) and asked us to buy postcards – proceeding to encourage us with the news that her mother was very ill.

"That's good", enthused John with an emphasis on the good.

"Good?" she replied incredulously.

"Yes", explained John. "Last week you told us that she was dead!"

Suddenly, a broad smile of comprehension and recognition spread over her pretty face and we got into conversation with her. Her name was Hoa (pronounced Waa and meaning flower) and she was living in a hostel in the city and sending money back to her family in a village some miles away. We learned that children have to pay to go to school in Vietnam – not a lot but, nevertheless, something we found rather strange in a socialist country.

(Thereafter, we met with Hoa quite often and would subsequently correspond with her after we returned to England. Her English was remarkably good from our first meeting and no doubt enhanced by her periodic encounters with tourists like us.)

Continuing our walk, we passed the 'Hanoi Hilton', the former prison where American prisoners-of-war were incarcerated in the 1970s during the Vietnam War. The site was now being redeveloped and only the outer wall remained giving a sinister twist to the modernity being created behind it. It seemed somehow eerie to think of the suffering that must have taken place within, all those years ago, whilst people were going about their everyday business outside.

(The recent unsuccessful American Republican presidential candidate, John McCain, who was shot down as a pilot during that conflict, was one of those imprisoned here from late 1967 until 1973).

It was much warmer today but slightly damp so the roads were filthy. Most people seem to wear totally inadequate sandals or jellies and so consequently have very dirty feet. Female peasants, who have come into the city from the villages to sell various items of produce, walk with small, hurried steps that demonstrate the weight of the two baskets bouncing up and down on either end of a long bamboo pole carried over one shoulder. They can even make fires in the bottom of their baskets on a layer of silver foil and cook on top. Today is Sunday but the traffic seems no different from all the other days.

Crouching at the side of the road seems to be a national pastime with whole families grouping together – some sitting on tiny plastic stools – to eat and chat. We really feel in control when we cross the road now and pay scant attention to the pedestrian traffic lights when we see them. Why they bother with a 'green man', goodness knows since it's only possible to half cross the road before the lights change and, more importantly, traffic ignores such things unless a policeman is around! At every major junction we saw a policeman who seemed to be acting purely as a spectator. As we progressed along the street little children and a few adults call out in genuinely friendly fashion, "Hello, how are you?" We really feel that we are novelty value for all and sundry but always respond with a smile and a reply of some sort which usually reduces the children to a severe and collective case of the giggles. Walking is something that involves great care and attention with continuous glancing down, not for the UK reasons when you might step in something that Fido has deposited, but because one is constantly in danger of breaking an ankle if you put your foot down any of the holes in the pavement. A comparison with the Mad Max films sprang to mind; we couldn't be sure whether 'civilisation' had been and gone leaving remnants from the past or whether it was just slow arriving. A sense of gloom pervades as we think of the lifestyle that people are happy to accept here but, of course, it is all they know at present. We returned to the cocoon that is our quiet, safe room at 12.30pm and were happy to relax on our own – shutting away the noisy world outside. To while away the time we looked through a book of baby names that we had brought from England and tried to shortlist some favourites. Hopefully, this wasn't tempting fate!

12

... and Waiting

Monday 22nd January

Again, not a good night's sleep for either of us. Breakfast at 8.30am: bread and a two-egg omelette, cheese and coffee. I found mine quite palatable with condensed milk but John still has his black. We went out an hour later and tried, for interest's sake, to locate Chien's house which was not far from the hotel and close to the railway station. We were interested to observe that the Vietnamese for railway station was *ga* – presumably reflecting the previous French influence on this country (gare). Eventually found what we were looking for but could see little as we didn't like to venture into the little alleyway that seemed to lead to her home. It appeared to be an apartment in an older style building. We carried on past rows of army surplus supplies following the Vietnamese tradition we had previously discovered of grouping together shops selling the same goods. We turned down a side road on the left and stopped to watch a train go by where the railway traversed the road. A railway official in a grey suit and peaked hat wheeled the barrier out to block off our section of the road and then repeated the exercise on the opposite side of the road. Traffic stopped, bikes and mopeds had the option of using a ramped bridge to go round which many did. Eventually, a very long and very old-looking train passed carrying a full complement of passengers. To one side of us a small group of men were eating and playing cards whilst sheltering under a tarpaulin.

We meandered along a rough track round a residential area and discovered a small outdoor market. A table of raw meat laid out under a grubby shelter caught our eye – no refrigeration here! Further on we encountered an industrial area where blacksmiths were busy on the side of the road and outside their various units apparently making wrought iron gates and other such items. New houses built in 1977 were mixed in with older shack-style properties giving the whole area an air of decayed optimism. Again, we were a source of interest, curiosity and occasional amusement to all we saw.

Returned via the same route to the hotel at 11.15am, made coffee and spent the rest of the day in the comparative comfort of our room sleeping and reading. Today was the day for the syphilis test result and Dr Rafi was able to confirm on the phone that it was negative. Hurrah! One more hurdle surmounted. No luck with the British Embassy since they told us that there were no English newspapers anywhere in Hanoi although we could try the Vietnamese Trade Office. We amused ourselves by making silly remarks and joking about our situation which helped to ease the tension. John creased me up by saying that if they hadn't done it already we could have written a book, the only difference would have been that this time Jill Morrell was incarcerated in Beirut with John McCarthy! Another thought had us speculating that if we ever got back to England with the baby we could placate Social

Services and their ethnic policy by adopting the various aspects of life we could see around us. We imagined a meal cooked on the pavement – dog of course!

Still no sign of the laundry we put out on Thursday despite having already paid for it. The bin might have been a cheaper option! Sweet and sour pork for our evening meal and then spent an hour chatting to the French. The phone rang and Chien explained we need an important document from the British Embassy that we must collect tomorrow. Both spent the rest of the night worrying as to how this might be achieved so very little sleep for either of us.

Tuesday 23rd January

Both up early and John rang Chien again to find out exactly what was needed. Apparently, the Vietnamese require a document signed on behalf the British government stating that we have permission to adopt. This could well be a huge fly in the ointment for us but there's no way around it. Managed some breakfast but both felt rather sick with anxiety. We walked to the Embassy and were there by 9am. An imposing-looking colonial building with an armed Vietnamese guard in a sentry box at the gate. We explained to a Vietnamese secretary what we needed, paid forty dollars and a letter was eventually produced signed by the Vice-Consul. Couldn't believe our luck as we rushed to Chien's office and collected her by taxi to take the document to the legalisation office. Queued for what seemed ages only to be told that it didn't have the correct wording. We were very concerned but nothing for it but to return to the Embassy and try again. This time Chien came with us but she had little success with the same secretary, got rather cross and left to wait outside leaving us to our own devices! John also was very close to losing his temper at this point and we seemed to up against a brick wall.

We hung around until John was eventually able to buttonhole a European member of staff who happened to pass through the reception area. She turned out to be an Australian member of staff, Lyn McDiarmid, and John explained to her the problem we were facing. Lyn was immediately sympathetic and went off to "see what I can do and would you please come back after lunch".

We returned to the hotel feeling very down and thought about packing everything in. This was an enormous stumbling block for us and we knew that if we couldn't successfully sort it out there would be no baby and no adoption. Despair hung between us in that small room and 2pm saw us back again at the Embassy.

A comparatively short while later Lyn came into the reception area with a new letter that contained some small but significant changes to the original. 'Wish to adopt' had been replaced by 'are able to adopt' which gave the British seal of approval as far as the Vietnamese were concerned. The letter also stated that, under United Kingdom law, John and I were 'entitled to apply for permission to bring a Vietnamese child into the United Kingdom for adoption'. Furthermore, 'the British Embassy would be grateful for any assistance which could be given' to us.

We waited, hearts in mouth, for another forty minutes for the letter to be signed by Deborah Ratcliffe, the Vice-Consul, still concerned that she might not be happy to do so but, at last, with the document in our hands, we were able to ring Chien and meet her again to walk back to the legalisation office. It had closed at 11.30am for the day but, luckily, she knew a lady who we could collect on the way. No problems this time and at 4pm, after parting with a further fifteen dollars, we had a legalised copy in our hands. At last, after all the anxieties of the day, we felt on a complete high. Things were looking up at long last.

Back at the hotel we chatted to the French about our problems. Chien had told us that we would need to go to the town of Ha Bac tomorrow to sign the adoption papers, a welcome break in our routine. During the evening a fax arrived from Sue Loveday, a real boost to our morale. We were so glad that it had come now and not earlier amidst the problems of the day. Chien arrived later in the evening to collect the form telling us that there was, after all, no need to go to Ha Bac tomorrow. A pity, we were both looking forward to the change of scenery which would have broken up the day for us. We passed over a small present of chocolates for the lady who had helped us today, which seemed the right thing to do. Spent the evening chatting to Jacqueline and Antoine who have a big day tomorrow, a meeting at the Justices Office. Saw the film 'Bodyline' on TV India, enjoyable and a semblance of normality in a very stressful day.

Wednesday 24th January

Another day! Had breakfast at 9.15am. Hard boiled eggs but no egg cups, only some small liqueur glasses which the tiny eggs often fell into. Have started playing cards to help pass the time. Had a massive tidy up in our room, John rewriting the labels for the blue boxes in readiness for the return journey. I'm sure this made him feel closer to going home!

At lunchtime Chien rang to say that it was the day at the office for the 'warm clothes' sale and that we could kit out the entire family for thirty five dollars. Were we interested? Had to say yes as we didn't want to rock the boat. Still don't know what the rules of this game are or, indeed, what the game is! Asked if we could hand them over ourselves when we visit the family. Went out for our usual walk to the lake. Three money-changing women were stationed outside the Post Office. They appeared to offer a good rate then tried to short-change John. Not a good idea! During all the haggling I sat by the lake and was asked to take photos of some young Vietnamese girls with their camera. They were very friendly and keen to practise their English. Nearby were some western-style shops selling videos and cameras. We inquired about the possibility of buying a camcorder with a customer helping to translate for us. Obviously a good price but as they were bought into the country from Hong Kong and no tax was paid it seemed no instructions were available either! Not a situation we felt like buying into. We wandered down side roads not previously explored, found St Joseph's cathedral, vast and very ornate and a tribute to French architecture. All the time we were accosted by postcard sellers *et cetera* wanting us to buy their wares. We returned to the sanctuary of our room. A day of no highs but no lows either.

Thursday 25th January
Another day looming with no real structure ahead. Today the eggs were so small they all fell into the 'egg cup', a source of huge amusement to us. We stayed in our room all morning, watched World Cup tennis from Australia and attempted the crossword from one of the old Times newspapers we had brought with us from that other world. Went out at 1.30pm to 61, Trant Tien, where the Caos' English-speaking cousin, Mme Nyget, worked in a gift shop. No lights were on but she explained that they go out at the same time everyday due to a power cut but if we return tomorrow she will take us to her company's second shop. On the other side of the road we saw a policeman dismiss a street seller – grabbing her two tin pots containing hot charcoal, emptying them into the gutter along with

the sweet corn she was cooking and making her move on. Selling in the street was obviously not allowed but, after he had gone, the pots were retrieved! We saw one large colonial-style shop selling hardware. There was a mezzanine floor inside and everything looked absolutely filthy. Nothing looks as though it has been touched or repaired since the French left in 1954. Hairdressers' shops are interesting, they all look very unkempt with cracked mirrors, broken, dirty floors and no back basins. We have seen one big one on Hang Bong that appears to be very overstaffed. Usually twelve people in the shop and of those six or seven are often playing cards by the window. The other style of hairdresser is the *al fresco* kind, a street cutter with a chair placed in front of a mirror hung on a wall or a tree! We assume that 'Cat Toc' written on the wall meant gents' hairdresser.

In front of the lake we watched as the Power Company building received a 'make over'; the vast front wall was being painted with a small roller whilst small tiles were being stuck onto a low wall in front of the flower garden. How strange to spend so much time on something so minor when so many more important things need doing. We visited the shops in Hang Gai Street where most of the silk and clothing items were being sold – maybe we will buy something small tomorrow. Back at the hotel I met Jacqueline as arranged yesterday and we went to see a baby basket that she had been told about. It was eighteen dollars and not really very suitable so I left without buying it. John was not too well in the evening and went to bed early. At 1.30am (6.30pm in the UK) we woke and rang Gill, our first contact with home and lovely to hear her voice. A real lifeline and a link with civilisation. Sleep was difficult afterwards.

* * *

Friday 26th January
So tired again and little to get up for. Had breakfast with the French but John really rough with a stomach bug and a bad back. Went out from 1.30pm to 3pm mainly to visit the bank and to have another look for a baby basket. Found two in a shop near the lake that will do – much cheaper than the other but there seems little point in buying anything until we know what is going on. We saw Hoa again, took her photo and bought two cards from her, our first.

John was anxious to return and went straight to bed. I went out on my own as I couldn't bear the thought of being cooped up any longer especially as John was asleep. I went in a new direction down Phung Hung St and explored the area between Hang Gai and the railway where there were dozens of small back streets. At first I felt rather brave being out on my own but at no point did I ever feel threatened or vulnerable as I might have done in a big western city. Eventually I found a large indoor market laid out on three floors. Outside there were several small units selling various items of western foods. Then I saw them! Each shop had two or three slightly rusty tins of Heinz baked beans. In fact, it looked as though the various units had split a case between them – which I'm sure they had.

Unfortunately, I had no money with me so I made a quick dash back to the hotel and dragged John back with me to see. We bargained and eventually got two tins for three dollars (the grand sum of £1 each and a small fortune for the Vietnamese). John was ecstatic, his dream food for the past several days and the only thing he could stomach at the moment.

We returned and whilst I consumed pork and tomatoes John was in his element with baked beans and a little bread. Jacqueline and Antoine have told us that they are leaving tomorrow as they have found a better hotel, a disappointment to us but we are locked into staying here since we have no wish to upset Chien.

Saturday 27th January

The strain of all this waiting without any idea about what will happen next and, more importantly, when it will happen is really starting to get to John. He likes to have some degree of control of a situation and to understand what is happening. At the moment, we are totally in the dark. What are we waiting for and when will it happen? The answers to both these questions are a complete mystery. He is determined to go to the Justice Department and find out what the system entails. I think it's a bad idea. So does Jacqueline. John cannot eat any breakfast so we leave early for Cat Linh where the Department is located. Apparently they don't work Saturdays but we were able to find someone who spoke English and he was able to explain a little more. He also said a decision from Ha Bac regarding an adoption can take one or two months. This seemed to satisfy John somewhat in that Chien was not keeping us waiting unnecessarily but the thought of so long a wait is impossible to contemplate. I wished desperately that he hadn't mentioned her name and am worried that he has interfered stupidly. I only hope it doesn't get back to her or create any problems. We walked to Ho Chi Min's mausoleum but both that and the museum were closed. John's back is really bad today. As we arrived back at the hotel we were just in time to see a duck having its throat cut on the pavement opposite. Its time was obviously up and dinner ready to be served. Scant regard is given to animal welfare here, they are a source of food and little else. Most things are kept live until the last possible moment due to the lack of refrigeration and so it is not unusual to see live chickens hanging upside down on the handlebars of a bike or to see a live pig trussed up and on its back on the back of a motorbike on its way to market. Presumably, anything that isn't sold can then be taken home again for sale on another day.

After playing cards, we went out mid afternoon and walked through the Old Quarter to the Cau Long Bien bridge. We crossed part way over; very few cars to be seen but a good view of the Red River. The muddy banks are not developed and it's obviously a poor area with a few small boats tied up. As we wandered through the side streets we noticed quite a few small hotels interspersed amongst the old buildings. Mostly narrow but one, in particular, stood out since it was the equivalent of five shops wide yet next to the oldest building we had seen to-date. Since these were all in a terrace I can't imagine how they managed to demolish and rebuild without the older ones collapsing.

Back to the hotel in time to receive a call from Chien. She had no more news but had we been to the Justice Department today? The jungle drums obviously work very efficiently here! I back-pedalled and the moment passed safely. She told us that 'maybe' we could have the baby on Tuesday but the family is concerned because the weather is so cold. This brought a mixture of both alarm and joy since Tuesday is so close. At 9pm my brother, Ian, rang from England to tell us that my cousin's husband had died. I felt an increased sense of isolation from events taking place so far away that I would normally have been very involved in. This sadness inevitably added to the general sense of gloom I was experiencing as I realized I would not even be able to go to the funeral.

Sunday 28th January
Got up late and, for once, I slept well but John is becoming increasingly agitated by the lack of action. He feels

that it might be worth trying to put pressure on Chien by inventing an illness for my mother which could necessitate us having to rush home to visit her in hospital. I made no comment but secretly felt this was a very bad idea. Being here is exactly like being in a permanent state of limbo. No rush, no urgency for anything. I guess that's how they operate in hot countries but it's so hard for us to get used to.

Another long day to fill. At least John was able to eat his beloved beans with some egg. Went out at 11.20am and walked to the West Lake some three kms away. It was a lovely area and obviously used to seeing tourists. Unfortunately, the persistence of the beggars and street sellers are becoming extremely irritating and detract from the pleasure of the walk. A man was wading out to catch winkles with a net whilst his wife sorted them on the promenade. As we passed a small hotel we decided to enquire as to the tariffs and were told fifty dollars for a week. The room we were shown was clean and it all looked superior to ours. Moving away from the lake we passed a sort of shanty town area and saw rows of joss sticks being laid out to dry on beds two feet high. Elsewhere there were dogs in cages, no doubt destined for the food chain as someone's next meal. No pets these! We turned right and discovered we were in gravestone-makers street. Here we were able to watch as they chiselled a picture and likeness into the stone as well as an inscription. How talented they are! Coffins were clearly on display. All rather macabre!

A little further on and back towards the city centre we came upon the very grand Metropole Hotel in Ngo Quyen Street close by the lake. It had been built in 1901 in the French colonial style and was described as 'having a rich history and a tradition of welcoming ambassadors, writers, heads of state and entrepreneurs'. It had 363 rooms and suites with a beautiful interior garden. We ventured in, happy to see other Europeans and to be in surroundings that felt more familiar to us. We enquired the price of the Sunday lunchtime buffet which, at 19 dollars per head, was rather more than we could really afford. The unknown length of our stay in Vietnam was beginning to have us look at every penny. A daily buffet at 7 dollars 50 cents looked excellent value as was afternoon tea at 5 dollars. We elected to have two coffees and two pieces of cheesecakes from the counter and sat back in comfort to listen to the live music and to watch the many Europeans, several of whom appeared also to be adopting Vietnamese babies. A half hour later the bill arrived – 19 dollars and 33 cents! We both nearly collapsed since John had only 13 dollars on him! On closer inspection it seemed that the cakes were a huge six dollars each and we hadn't taken into account the service charge and tax. John asked for the manager, a very pleasant Frenchman, who listened politely to our request that we return later with more money. In the meanwhile, John offered to leave his watch behind – and told me later that he had thought of leaving me as security! But the manager would not hear of it and insisted that we were his guests for the entire amount. I have never seen John so embarrassed or red-faced! We both felt very relieved but, in fact, we never went back there again!

At the lake we saw Hoa, the post card seller who, we discovered, lives with friends in a kind of dormitory close to the river bridge and sends money home to her family in a province not far from Hanoi. We passed the one-armed beggar on Hang Gai who was especially persistent and could obviously spot Europeans at a considerable distance. Back at the hotel we played cards all evening and had a phone call from Gill at 9pm. So nice to hear a familiar voice and get all the news from home.

97

13

And Now We Are Three

Monday 29th January

We found it helpful each day to try to have some sort of project or task to fulfil to help pass the time. Both of us are normally busy people and this enforced idleness is something we find extremely difficult to cope with. Yesterday we had bought a set of postcards showing old views of Hanoi as it was when occupied by the French many decades ago. We decided to track down these buildings and take present-day photographs to show the changes and set out to do so with a mixed degree of success as some buildings were now no longer in existence. The cyclo 'boys' were very persistent today, a real nuisance. We also managed to buy two T-shirts in Hang Gai after some bargaining which I loath but John enjoys. John is getting really annoyed about the continuing delays and persuaded me to ring Chien to hurry things along and press the point about the need to get home rather urgently. We both feel very down since nothing appears to be happening and John makes it clear that unless we push to speed things up he is not willing to stay indefinitely. We are also very conscious that there is only a fortnight left on our visas, particularly as we are increasingly aware that they are non-extendable.

When we finally return to the hotel at 5pm there has been a phone call from Chien to say that we can collect the baby TODAY and she will be collecting us in a taxi at 5.30pm.

We hadn't eaten since breakfast and now dinner was off, too.

John returned the call saying how worried I was in case he has to return on Saturday and she is most sympathetic. She arrived quickly and we had little time to prepare ourselves. My hair needed washing, I had no make up on and I felt a real mess. So much for having plenty of time to prepare for what was, in reality, a momentous occasion. All the wasted time of the last ten days and now here we were in a blind panic. I barely had time to grab a few things I thought I might need for the baby before we piled into the taxi that Chien had arrived in and, travelling east over the Red River, we left the city for the first time since we had arrived.

It took an hour to travel to Ha Bac and, since it was 'rush hour', the roads were horrendously busy. Goodness knows how there aren't more accidents. Bikes and motorbikes are often without lights and the standard of driving leaves a lot to be desired. We passed paddy fields on both sides of the road but soon it became too dark to see very much. Eventually, we arrived at the house of an intermediary who was assisting in the adoption and are told that we must wait whilst she and Chien go on to the village to collect the baby. We had time only to give Chien our camera in the hope that she might get some photos of the family. We were then left with this second woman's husband who spoke no English and their 14 year old son who could speak only a little. Soon he disappeared to do some homework and we passed an increasingly anxious two hours waiting and trying to imagine what was happening out in the countryside. Had the parents changed their minds? When 'push came to shove', could they really do it and give up their child?

The room we waited in had little comforts and a motorbike stood in one corner. But it possessed the most amazing TV and stereo unit – far superior to anything we had at home. John needed to go to the toilet and told me later that the conditions in the corridor behind were very primitive. These strong contrasts are the things I find most fascinating about this country; evolution is developing at a racing gallop without the steady build up of any form of infrastructure. The juxtaposition of new and old is astonishing.

Finally, at 8.30pm, the women returned. Chien was grinning madly as she thrust this tiny bundle into my arms. This really was it! The moment we had been waiting years for! Our own baby!

The emotion was so overwhelming that I felt almost stupefied and unsure of what to do next. I could only clutch her like an idiot as someone took a photo with our camera. The baby had a black mark on her forehead which, we were told, had been given as a sign of leaving. Apparently, the family had all been very upset but had been keen for the photos to be taken. The baby was wrapped in a pink rug and, sitting with John in the back of the taxi, I held her tightly all the way back to the hotel trying not to dwell on how the family must be feeling at this moment.

It was 9.40pm when we arrived back at the hotel. We had not eaten all day so we placed the baby on the bed and went back downstairs to eat with Chien. Halfway through the baby began to cry and I began my first duties as a new mother! Chien had told us that the intermediary will try to rush things through and also that the family would like a

TV as a gift. This is something that we will be able to sort out ourselves and will give us something to do in the days ahead. After she left we needed to organise ourselves since we had been unable to prepare for the new arrival earlier. The baby was bound to be hungry and I had never so much as made up a bottle before. I was able to do it reasonably quickly, reading the instructions as I went. I then gave her the first of many bottles which, luckily, she took quite well. What I would have done if she had refused, I have no idea. I assumed she had been totally breastfed up until now and that the bottle might cause her problems but all was fine – thank goodness! – since I was in enough of a panic already. We carefully took off all the clothes she was wearing – the same garments as last week – which smelt quite badly and then gave her a first bath in our large one. The dirt was ingrained and the tiny mite was, by now, very upset and screaming furiously. We made a temporary bed by placing one of the baby mattresses we bought with us inside an empty suitcase. The start of our first night as a family.

Nothing seemed real!

Tuesday 30th January

What a night! It seemed as if we had only slept for about an hour since the baby wouldn't settle which, I guess, was quite understandable. A feed at 3 o'clock and then at 8am after which we brought her into bed between us, with some reservation, and all then slept until noon! Thinking about it, this was probably what she was used to. Getting organised and seeing to her seemed to take forever and it was some time before we got round to the important job of making tea! Finally, at 2.45pm, we were, at last, ready to go out. The white snowsuit was miles too big for this tiny mite who, at three months, weighed only 6lbs but it was all I had. The garment seemed to continue for at least six inches past her toes, if not further. The hat, again huge, so one of hers was put on instead, an acid yellow item that bore a remarkable resemblance to a mini tea cosy. It certainly made us laugh.

Our only means of transporting her was in a baby sling and the smaller of the two we had bought with us was ideal. After adjustments she was in and I carried her in front of me on my chest, an immensely proud feeling that I'm sure all new parents experience. Far from disliking it, the motion of the sling made her fall asleep very quickly and this pattern was to be repeated whenever we ventured out with her in this way. Our aim today was to price TV sets which seemed to take ages.

Eventually we found 'TV Street' and managed to locate what we were looking for. We had suddenly become a special sort of attraction today and the baby sling gained many curious glances. Several people actually stopped us on the pavement to peer at the baby deep inside with men also taking an interest. 'Ah, Vietnam' was the verdict time after time and we soon suspected that the locals were expecting to see a European baby. Although we couldn't understand what they were saying it seemed that the bridge of the baby's nose was of a considerably attractive shape and the fact that the back of her head was rounded was also viewed with much admiration. We later discovered that Vietnamese babies spend a lot of time lying on their backs with the result that their heads tend to get somewhat flattened. This clearly had not happened to our baby.

We also surmised that the word 'Vietnamese' didn't exist as the baby was referred to as 'Vietnam' on every occasion.

On our return to the hotel, we learned that Antoine and Jacqueline had called by so we rang them later and made arrangements to visit them the next day. Our lack of equipment is creating all sorts of problems, especially relating to our ability to support the baby. We have no choice but to use either the sling or the suitcase and so, during our evening meal, leave her upstairs asleep whilst we eat quickly, taking turns to check on her at regular intervals. It was 1am before she finally settled and then a short sleep for us until 5.30am. The difficulties of coping in a confined space where we are all on top of one another is horrendous but somehow we settle into a routine far more quickly than I would ever have imagined. It is really a case of just getting on with it and doing the best that we can. We are very conscious that the baby is well aware that she is in an alien environment and the current situation is as strange for her as it is for us. However, she has 'survived' so far in conditions that are certainly far from ideal so she must be reasonably resilient!

Our visas expire two weeks today and are non-extendable.

Wednesday 31st January
Today, we borrowed a baby bath from the hotel and gave her what was, probably, her first ever 'real' bath. The quick attempt on the first night had not really counted. We balanced the bath on the small coffee table and sat on the end of the bed so that neither of us had to lean over. Both of us have dodgy backs from old sporting injuries, John from rugby and me from hockey. The ingrained dirt will take many such baths before it finally disappears, even her hands are filthy. The crevices in the skin around her neck are a particular problem and it will be some time before I will be able to clean that area satisfactorily without hurting her. She really hated being washed and caused a tremendous amount of noise proving that, at least, her lungs are working well.

(We were later told that the reason her parents had chosen to put her up for adoption rather than her sister was because she had the louder 'voice' and would therefore be able to make herself heard the better!)

The morning was spent washing clothes and seeing to the baby. I can't believe what a full time job it was already turning out to be. However do parents manage to do anything else? I tried to put the thought of how I would cope once we returned home out of my mind. After all, that was surely tempting fate.

It was time to decide on the baby's name. We have previously spent many hours lying on the bed each compiling our own individual list of possible names. I am sure that all prospective parents probably do the same. We had eventually read our suggestions to one another whilst the other proceeded to dismiss each offering in turn. We both rather liked Ellie-Mae until we realised that it had a familiar ring because it was the name of Nigel Pargetter's cow in The Archers on BBC radio and so yet another name went onto the discard pile. So, today, we decided that the baby was officially to be called Ellen Frances the same as John's maternal grandmother and names we both particularly liked. Her parents had given her the name of their village – Vu Duong (pronounced 'voo zoying' to our ear) – to take away with her and we have decided to retain that as a link with her past. Ellen Frances Vu Duong Ley-Morgan. What a mouthful for such a tiny scrap.

We went out for a couple of hours in the afternoon for a change of scenery and introduced Ellie to Hoa. She was very taken with the baby and the other children came crowding round. Finally, we returned to the hotel and were ready to receive Jacqueline and Antoine who arrived with a super little baby 'gro' in peppermint green, with ears like a rabbit. It was the first garment of its kind that I had seen in Hanoi and they had done well to track it down. Unfortunately, it was far too large and it would be another nine months before it fitted – by which time Ellie would be too old to be wearing such an item! The lack of any such items in the local shops meant we have had no opportunity to buy clothes in smaller sizes and have had to make do with the very limited supply of tiny clothes we had brought with us from England. Another reason why I seem to be constantly washing!

The French stayed for about an hour and a half during which time Ellie behaved impeccably at her first tea party. She was a big hit or, to be more accurate, a small hit since she'll never be a big anything! By way of a celebration we decided, after they had left, to visit the one and only pizza restaurant that we have discovered not far from the hotel and run by two young Australian lads. The thought of European food encouraged us to eat early and, on arrival, we found the place virtually empty and sat down at a table of our choice.

Looking around the room John immediately recognised a face at a nearby table as that of Michael Eavis, the founder of the Glastonbury pop festival and, in the grand scale of things, virtually a neighbour of ours at Weston-super-Mare! First Mike Roe on TV and now Michael Eavis in the flesh. What incredible co-incidences! We felt so far from home yet we have now experienced two examples of how small the world has become. John went over and introduced himself and discovered that Michael and his wife were taking a year out from the annual Festival and, as guests of Oxfam, were being shown how some of the money they had raised for charity was being spent in the Third World. A quick chat more than made our day and provided another much-needed link with 'our world'. It was a super evening and Ellie did not stir in her sling whilst

I circumnavigated her with pizza and salad whilst John demolished a tasty spaghetti bolognaise. On our return, a phone call from Mum contributed to our good mood and I was able to share our exciting news about Ellie which she was thrilled to receive. The end of a very satisfactory day!

Thursday 1st February

We are both incredibly tired since Ellie did not settle all night and so sleep for us was almost non-existent. John went out on his own in the morning and tried to buy a TV but no luck. I stayed behind and tried to sleep but was unable to do so since Ellie would still not settle. We both took a stroll in the afternoon to relieve the tedium and, as usual, Ellie was asleep in no time in her sling. Clearly the motion is much to her liking. We hope this will not mean another bad night. The roads were as crowded and noisy as always and walking not easy since there were so many obstacles to negotiate. Sometimes it might be a family having a meal or even someone performing their ablutions, but always one has to skirt round motorbikes and bicycles that took pride of place parked on the pavement. An area near the kerb is often marked off by a white dotted line especially set aside as a parking zone. Pedestrians seem to take second place here, the antithesis of the western world! Occasionally, a small hole has been dug and a white tile inserted in place of paint giving an air of permanence to the status quo. Unfortunately, the denoted zone is often not adhered to and the parking creeps closer to the shop front. A tortuous route then has to be made to negotiate all these vehicles which usually means that, in desperation, one gives up and walks in the road, a far quicker if not safer option! This at least means that the danger of breaking an ankle by stepping in a hole in the pavement, where underground gullies have been exposed, is negated.

We meandered around the lake and back through Hang Gai where we treated ourselves to some silk scarves which we thought would make inexpensive presents to take back home. This process in itself became a major battle as we were quickly pounced on by any shopkeeper who thought we might be in danger of not parting with some money. Auntie Wainwright in *Last of the Summer Wine* came frequently to mind! Unfortunately, this constant pressure from shopkeepers has quite the opposite effect to what they were trying to achieve and time and time again we turned away not wishing to be hassled, the desire to buy diminishing in inverse proportion to the amount of attention we received. At 5.30pm we gave Ellie her second bath which caused just as much protest as the first. A very fatty evening meal of sweet and sour pork which I coped with but John hated. Little on TV but at least Ellie was quiet all evening.

Friday 2nd February

What joy! Probably had six hours sleep, maybe more. We went out early to Van Mieu and also met the daughter which was good since translation suddenly became possible. They wanted us to visit the Temple of Literature with them the following week but we fervently hope we will not still be here! We discovered at breakfast what the loudspeaker announcements which we continually hear in the street were saying. Apparently, the 7am and 4pm 'broadcasts' are a means of relaying information in the city. Pairs of loudspeakers are attached high up on lampposts at intervals of twenty yards. The latest news item concerns the prominence of English language signs. The Communist government is telling people that these need to be removed and replaced by Vietnamese signs and if they wish to show an English sign it has to be displayed in smaller writing and sited in a subsidiary position. Our hotel sign had been changed two days ago and everywhere we have seen sign writers and carpenters busy replacing old and erecting new signs. This year the country is celebrating sixty-six years of communist rule and banners are prevalent across all the major roads. We somehow suspect a link here with the move to down-grade Western influence by reducing the prominence of signs written in English.

Whilst we were out we saw many indications of the approaching Tet, the Vietnamese New Year, with numerous preparations taking place. Trees have been painted white from the ground to a height of about three feet which, we later learnt, is to ward off evil spirits and to denote strength. Banners in red and yellow festoon the streets and much cleaning and tidying up appears to be going on around the lake. We collected photographs which had been developed and printed at a shop near the lake and then saw Hoa with whom we chatted. She said that she would like to write to us after we go home and told us more of her circumstances: it costs her twenty US dollars a month to go to school and the postcards she sells belong to an agent. If she were to earn enough she could, perhaps, buy her own supply.

Back at the hotel we busied ourselves with small chores and then rang Chien. The bad news was that there will be no ceremony before next Wednesday and to dispel the air of gloom that settled over us we ventured out for another pizza. Later, we were surprised to see Hanoi featured on the World News and gained a little more insight into the mystery that surrounded us. Apparently, the government has ordered the taking down of all Western hoardings and advertisements since they are considered 'decadent' and a demonstration in Hanoi was shown although this was nothing we had first hand knowledge of. Again, the

TV featured nothing worth watching, more episodes of *MASH* not proving very diverting.

Saturday 3rd February

A very good night and Ellie woke only once to feed. She has proved to be a real sweetie and already we love her to bits. Anh, the receptionist, has taken to holding her whilst we have our breakfast and, for her, Ellie is always quiet. We spent the morning doing the inevitable chores confined in our small room whilst Ellie lay quietly on the bed. Routine seems to be the best way to survive; giving us a reason to get up and an order to the day. I have soon mastered the art of bottle making and, thankfully, the plastic jug I had the foresight to bring (or maybe it was on Sue's list of useful items?) enables me to make up sufficient feed for a day. The *pièce de résistance* was the disposable bottle system which works brilliantly. This consisted of a plastic bottle liner, with volume markings, which fits into an outer solid plastic tube. Reusable teats screw onto the top. Once I had the hang of how it works it has proved to be superb, relinquishing the need for any sterilising. One or two accidents in fitting has meant that, on more than one occasion, I have been amazed to see Ellie consume a whole bottle in double quick time, only to discover that most of it had leaked down her neck and she was soaked! Sod's Law – this usually happens just after she has been changed!

(In fact, the system was to prove so effective that when we returned to the UK I continued to use it despite the obvious difference in cost to the normal system – my excuse to John being that I needed to use up the supply of bags that I still had whilst secretly replenishing my stocks from local shops!)

Thankfully, I have brought a sufficient supply with me

and am always careful not to spoil any. The thought of trying to sterilize things in such a tiny space, with limited equipment, is more than I could cope with. We took our usual walk in the afternoon, thankful for a change of scenery, and discovered a shop selling coconut milk ice creams which, for 2,000 dong (14p), were delicious. The weather was warm and sunny and, for us, the temperature comfortable and pleasant. For a short time we could almost imagine that we are tourists on holiday, forgetting the turmoil and anxiety within us. We followed our usual route round the lake but no sign of Hoa today. The curiosity and interest of many Vietnamese, even small boys, followed us as we were pointed out and people vied to see the baby – still, probably, expecting to see a European child.

Today, February 3rd, is the sixty-sixth anniversary of Communism in Vietnam and the street loudspeakers are continuously playing music. We also saw a bandstand being set up by the lake for a performance, presumably later during the evening. Anh, the receptionist, had told us earlier that all the banners we have seen are for this occasion and nothing to do with Tet as we had at first surmised. We wandered into a road we hadn't visited before (Ly Quo Su) and discovered the Roman Catholic cathedral of St Joseph's. It is vast and beautiful inside with huge stained glass windows, a very calm and peaceful atmosphere after the noise and bustle of the streets outside. A tribute to the French colonial era and their architectural influence. As we left we saw a blind man, selling brushes, who had a small bell which jangled as he moved. I couldn't begin to imagine how he coped with so much traffic around and the state of the pavements which must surely be full of hidden dangers for him. We actually spotted one back road which had been recently tarmaced and commented on how well it had been done. I should have liked to have watched the process as I'm sure it would have been fascinating to see. On Trang Thi there was a site where a large building was slowly being demolished, mainly with mallets and one or two pneumatic drills. No large-scale demolition equipment here! Yesterday, we saw a delivery of scaffolding poles to the large building site at what was the 'Hanoi Hilton' prison – by cyclo!

Back in the peace, quiet and sanctuary of our room Ellie awoke from her three-hour sleep in the baby sling and was given a bath and nappy change, both of which she absolutely hated and so screamed with gusto. For the first time we saw her begin to suck the fingers on her right hand. (A trade mark that was to last some months until eventually in England, the resulting soreness brought the habit to a halt.) Noodles for our evening meal, filling and adequate.

14

The Fall Out With Chien

Sunday 4th February
A poor night. Ellie woke at 2am and it took nearly two hours to settle her and, consequently, we were both tired and snappy by morning. After breakfast we went back to bed and managed an extra couple of hours sleep. In the afternoon we saw Hoa by the lake and did some shopping for small items to take home as gifts. We picked out some T-shirts which are all hand-embroidered by local Vietnamese women and costing less than £2 each. The actual shirts (which we suspected were imported from China) were of poor quality and the sizing often erratic in contrast to the wonderful designs and workmanship by the locals. Hang Gai Street, where the silk shops are situated, is almost becoming a no-go area as we are accosted by beggars and street traders – not to mention cyclo drivers. We both found it rather tiring and this, coupled with the constant cacophony of the tooting of horns and the general noise, is severely undermining our morale.

We wandered down a small side street and saw blood on the pavement with, close by, a bird whose throat had just been cut. It made me feel quite sick. We tried to find the French restaurant that Jacqueline and Antoine had previously told us about and tracked it down close to the Italian pizza restaurant but the prices were rather high for our now meagre budget. Instead, we ordered a pizza to be delivered to the hotel for 7.30pm which meant we didn't have to venture out again with Ellie and could eat whilst she lay in her cot – otherwise known as the medium-sized suitcase!

We returned to the hotel at 6.30pm with time to bath her before the pizza arrived but suddenly, at 6.50pm, Chien arrived, unannounced, in our room. I was rather embarrassed as we were in total chaos. Keeping the small room tidy is difficult at the best of times but now Ellie is with us the problem has magnified. Chien made several phone calls concerning the Leaving Ceremony during which time Ellie cried loudly and continuously. We both felt very much as though our personal space had been violated. In between calls her eyes were everywhere around the room.

"How much did John's jumper cost?"

Answer: a cheap one from a Weston store.

"What is in the blue boxes?" *et cetera.*

During this inquisition I was relieved to realise that I had put everything bought that afternoon away and so they were shielded from her prying eyes. We certainly didn't want to give her the impression that we had money to spare. Even the imminent delivery of the pizza seemed to be a threat. Finally, we were told, "Good news, the ceremony might be Friday or Saturday!"

At this point John exploded. We had been expecting to hear that the ceremony would be any day now and the dubious news that it wouldn't be for nearly another week, at the earliest, was too much for him. 'We have to go on Saturday,' he told her. 'We will have to leave the baby behind. There will be no job for me in England if I don't

113

return soon.' It all poured out in one long tirade of frustration and pent up anger. I was in tears and Chien stormed out with the passing shot that we could do it on our own from now on and she would no longer be involved.

God, it was absolutely dreadful.

I felt that, after all this waiting, we had blown the whole thing since it would probably be impossible to go forward on our own. There is nothing to be done but for me to ring her at home, swallow my pride and attempt to pour oil on troubled waters. I hate speaking to her on the phone since I still have difficulty understanding her but I can see that there is no other course of action available. I think this must be one of our lowest points. John realises that his way is not going to work and the more one tries to bully these people or speed things up the more entrenched they become. If we are to succeed we will have to play the game their way or not at all.

I grovelled. I apologised and finally I was able to talk her round but, from that point on, all future negotiations were between Chien and me with John taking a diplomatic back seat. I think he feels totally at sea, finding himself in a position where the tenuous grasp he had on controlling the situation has finally snapped. He is, at last, able to see that if Ellie is ever going to return to the UK with us our approach will have to alter radically. In some ways, this resigned acceptance has made things easier for me as I no longer feel that I am fighting on two fronts. Whether Ellie will ultimately become ours or not is certainly in the balance but we are going to give it every shot we can! The pizza arrived, almost forgotten in the mêlée and we made a token effort at eating it, neither of us with much enthusiasm or enjoyment. Today has been one that both of us wish to forget and the general air of depression is only marginally relieved by a phone call from Gill at 9pm. We will certainly not be leaving on Saturday as planned and, tomorrow, another visit to the Singapore Airline office will be required to change our flight reservations once again.

Monday 5th February

The start of another day which began with us both tired since we were up with Ellie on several occasions during the night. Our routine followed the same course: chores, a sleep and then an escape route to the lake where we indulged in a chocolate ice this time. We discovered more tonic to go with our gin at the bargain price of about 3,000 dong (30p) and it was Schweppes, too! In Tran Thi we wandered into an exhibition about Thailand, celebrating fifty years of rule by the reigning monarch. It was most interesting and contained English subtitles – a bonus for us. We glanced at a few restaurant menus but will probably stick with the Pizzeria where, at least, we know what to expect when the bill arrives! Jacqueline has told us of their eating out experiences when they had seen live rats on three separate occasions, the last being on the rafters of the restaurant in which they were eating. On our return we gave Ellie another bath and again experienced what we now call 'nappy rage'. A simple meal of noodles for John and fish for me with the prospect of another episode of *Morse* to watch on TV. Probably a repeat we have previously seen but still a small step towards making us feel a little more at home.

Tuesday 6th February

Another day dawning. Is it possible that we are beginning to get used to the state of limbo we find ourselves in? Not a bad night but still feeds at 1am, 3.30am and 5.30am so both tired this morning. A two-hour sleep for all three of us after breakfast and then we went out at 2.30pm. Ellie gave me my first smile before we left. It was a magical moment! She really is an undemanding baby and we both are finding it so easy to bond with her. If it wasn't for the uncertainty of the circumstances we find ourselves in this could have been a wonderful time for us all to get to know one another. Certainly an opportunity that many dads rarely have with their new offspring. It was a beautiful day outside and we felt strangely relaxed as we circuited the lake. We paused to watch a cockfight between two hooded, scrawny little chickens cheered on by a small group of men squatting around them. No banners on view today, all have been taken down. Ellie slept the entire time we were out and received much admiration in the bank despite her comatosed state. More noodles for supper; better the devil you know and less danger of receiving a stomach upset!

Wednesday 7th February

A reasonable night but the 1am feed proved rather difficult as there was no electricity. I was just able to cope by giving Ellie her bottle in the bathroom, sitting on the toilet, where a small amount of light came in through the tiny window. As the power was off for more than one and a half hours it was impossible to see to change her. That had to wait. We managed about seven hours sleep but still had a nap for a couple of hours at lunchtime. This could become a habit! I suspect that some of our tiredness is due to the constant anxiety that surrounds us and which has now become a part of our lives. We had a lovely play with Ellie on the bed after her morning bath. She is a dear little soul but hates anything to do with being changed or cleaned. I suppose it is because it is so alien to the way she has been looked after up until now.

Our saunter out in the afternoon involved a visit to Singapore Airline to change our flight bookings, yet again.

The staff has been absolutely marvellous over this and so helpful. We saw a beggar with only one leg who was pulling himself along the ground whilst pushing a bowl in front of him. It was a busy junction too and made me feel quite desperately sad that someone would have to live like this. John suggested that the man might be a war veteran but we had no idea. We gave him some money but Chien later told us that the man would probably only spend it on drink. Who could blame him?

Noodles yet again for our evening meal. This regime is certainly good for the waistline if not for our general well being. John has lost a lot of weight and it's very noticeable.

Thursday 8th February

We all slept well but seemed to have little incentive to get up and so consequently were late down to breakfast. We both felt quite down since there had been no news from Chien since Sunday. With the clock slowly ticking away we are getting closer to the date when our visas will run out on Monday – now only four days away. A month had seemed such a long time when we first arrived but now here we are with only a few days left and that, we suspect, could well be a huge problem for us. If the Leaving Ceremony has any chance of taking place this weekend we would surely have heard by now but, there again, who knows what sort of warning we will get if our experience in collecting Ellie is anything to go by. I couldn't stop myself from having a little cry which was seen by Anh, the young receptionist. Jacqueline rang whilst we were eating to say that they had settled well into their new hotel but that she had a bad cold which meant she had been unable to visit her baby for the last four days. This made her feel rather down as well. At least we have Ellie with us and the saying 'possession is nine tenths of the law' is something we are firmly holding on to! Jacqueline's hotel is not far from here and we now have the phone number so can keep in touch.

Ellie is certainly thriving and taking her bottles well. If she misses one through being asleep she makes up for it by having two close together. After doing my chores I could put off the moment no longer and was just about to ring Chien, anxious that doing so might antagonise her, when Anh rang up to say that I (not we) had visitors. I left John in the room and went down to reception to find Chien with two American women, one husband and two Vietnamese girls around ten and eleven years of age who were each to be adopted. Since this was the first time I had seen her since 'the fight', it was a big hug and apology from me and a reunion that, hopefully, will take us one step closer to our goal. I explained about the imminent expiry of our visas and she promised to sort it out. Apparently, as we suspected, it was a very important matter so now more pressure is being piled on us by a situation we ourselves can do nothing to alter or influence. Chien asked for our passports but I couldn't make out what she was going to do with them. I went back to the room and brought them down along with Ellie to meet everyone and then returned upstairs whilst they all ate. We waited and waited expecting that Chien would speak to us again but eventually it became obvious that she had left without saying goodbye. With our passports! Our stomachs were churning and this latest development concerning the visas has made us both feel very jittery and vulnerable.

We walked to the lake where we bumped into Hoa who was, as always, very pleased to see us and Ellie, especially. The problem with the soon-to-expire visas has been the main topic of conversation between the two of us and we fantasised that police would appear at our room in just a few days time to escort us to the airport whilst

Ellie was taken from us. We are absolutely convinced that the regime, as we have come to view it, will not allow us to overstay our visit for any reason. We are both in deep despair at the prospect.

When we got back to the hotel we found that Chien had returned and was, it seemed, waiting for a telephone call. Eventually it came through but the news was bad. The ceremony cannot be before Monday or even Tuesday. Our earlier despair has been justified but John is suddenly being uncharacteristically philosophical about it all. He has, at last, come to accept that nothing we can do will change things and there is therefore no alternative but to put all thoughts of home and 'normal' life out of our minds and to go with the flow. If, in the process, he loses his training contract, so be it. Que sera, sera! A bath for Ellie, noodles, and a welcome phone call later from Gill. This is what our lives consist of. One day at a time.

Friday 9th February

Anh was explaining to us this morning about Tet which begins a week on Sunday. The celebration of the Vietnamese New Year. Apparently it is a time of great rejoicing for all Vietnamese and extends for a whole week in much the same way as Christmas nowadays does for us. People will return home to Vietnam from abroad to visit their families, others will leave to visit relatives now in other countries. Everything will shut down for the duration of Tet and we now realise that if we don't leave the country by Saturday 17th February we will have to wait for at least another seven days after that. Even if our funds will stretch to that (and they won't) we still have the enormous problem of the soon-to-expire visas.

Late again down to breakfast at 9.45am but at least Ellie had a good night and so did we. We had a long chat

119

with Anh on reception and learnt that Duan, the male receptionist, who spoke the best English of all the staff, had left as he was fed up at being asked to do so much at the hotel. Apparently he was thirty seven but looked no older than nineteen. We have previously been struck by how young the majority of adults looked. When we had first called into the bank it appeared to be staffed by schoolboys and schoolgirls! Anh had much to say about her Director at the hotel and also about Chien that was not always complimentary!

Back upstairs the phone went and Chien explained that the only way to extend our visa was to send a car to Ha Bac where they would confirm that we were in the middle of an adoption process. Naturally we must pay! Also, would we like to go to the West Lake with the Americans on Sunday? In order not to rock the boat or appear ungrateful I said yes, although not really wanting to go. I really couldn't see what else we could do, certainly concerning the visa. Jacqueline had told us that a tourist visa was not extendable unless the adoption process was underway. This is something that the British Embassy might normally be able to help with but that certainly was taboo for us. There is no way that we wish to draw their attention to us since the question of a visa for the baby (or lack of it!) might become an issue. We are both totally fed up whilst Ellie lay cooing on the bed, completely unaware of the tension surrounding her. I hope that one day she will appreciate everything that we are going through in order to become a family. With my chores done the rest of the day looms ahead completely empty. Sue Loveday, I reflect, was so lucky to have completed her adoption so quickly.

Tet is imminent and after a last-minute mad rush of people between city and countryside the internal structure within the country will remain suspended for a week while the rejoicing continues. Any chance of a Leaving Ceremony will be impossible during that time. Please, please PLEASE don't let us be here then. What is only a few more days in England will seem a lifetime for us here. All around us are the signs of the approaching festivities as we see Orange Blossom trees being ferried home on the backs of bicycles and motor bikes. They symbolise the start of the New Year and one has appeared in the hotel foyer. As the tightly closed buds begin to open our depression grows knowing that soon, when they are in full bloom, Tet will be upon us, effectively making us prisoners in time.

We left early for our walk to the lake. Again, it was warm and sunny and Hoa was on duty but today so sad as she had sold nothing. We shopped for dried milk powder and more baked beans, anything to give our existence a semblance of normality. Ellie appears to have a slight cold so no bath today. Again we asked for our meal to be sent up; it's so much easier than coping with Ellie when she's awake and us having nowhere to put her. We watched TV; *MASH* has become an almost favourite programme out of the limited choice we have, giving us that vital link to a more familiar world. Some of the best programmes are on during the day, the evenings not so good. We planned to watch the film *Honeymoon in Las Vegas* advertised on Star India for 9pm. We worked out that it should be 10.30pm here but didn't manage to find it so those calculations were all wrong and the mystery remained. Such a small thing to have missed it and yet we had been looking forward to it for days. Despondency again crept in. A *sotto voce* argument ensued so as not to wake Ellie concerning my arrangements for Sunday's visit to the lake. How was I going to get out of it since neither of us wanted to go? Why do I manage, time and time again, to get myself into corners? It's simply because I don't want to offend and don't know what the form is. Are we allowing ourselves to be manipulated or are our over-active imaginations seeing all sorts of machinations where none exist? Whilst feeding Ellie at 4am and watching the World Service news on TV we saw the details of the Irish bomb at Canary Wharf in London and heard the announcement of the end of the ceasefire agreement. So far away but still in our thoughts.

Saturday 10th February
A reasonable night for Ellie but I just don't seem to be able to feed her without getting milk all around her neck. At the moment it's a change of clothes per feed and with the time taken to dry I just don't have enough. All I can think of is that she will have to wear two of the bigger sets of clothes I have. The washing seems to be non-stop! Yesterday I spent some time looking to find alternative things but other than something that looked like a mini ski suit had no luck. If I could source cheap baby-gros I might yet make my fortune. Our (almost) silent argument is just about over. Oh, how I wish this process would speed up.

After doing my chores, another argument developed concerning my handing over our passports to Chien. It's now two days since we last saw them and you hear such awful stories about people losing passports, whilst we've handed ours over voluntarily. We went out at noon, both in a foul mood and doing something we had not done before which was take our frustrations out on each other. We saw a little girl selling sets of small Vietnamese hats who we had chatted to a few days ago. Today we bought three sets in different sizes, it will be something to hang in Ellie's room and a reminder of Vietnam (as if we needed one!). We bumped into Chien in a side street – how many bizarre coincidences are we going to encounter in this place? I know that, as cities go, Hanoi is quite small but there are still three million people here and this is the second time we've bumped into her in four weeks! We were relieved to hear that our passports had been left at the hotel. Panic over! Apparently, we will get the adoption papers from Ha Bac on Monday and the ceremony may be on Monday, maybe Tuesday. Funny, that sounds so familiar! She was also pleased to tell us that the police had rung to say that they think they had found her bike.

By the lake we found a photographer's shop and had Ellie's passport photos taken. Such a small thing but bringing nearer the hope of our eventual departure. John had to support Ellie' head with his hand whilst the photographer did his stuff. She is so small that it fitted neatly in his palm and is a picture we will always treasure. We avoided returning via Hang Gai and the hassle from the traders by turning into the Old Quarter. The smells that we encountered on our walks were many and varied: market smells, food cooking, occasional drain smells and some areas which were obviously used as public latrines. These later ones assaulted my nostrils in particular but John was spared all of the unpleasant ones since his sense of smell has been non-existent for quite a number of years now. However, he was dearly missing those newly-bathed baby smells that he remembered from years ago and that he knew I could now experience with Ellie.

We stopped a lady pushing a bike that was laden down with painted china vases of all shapes and sizes and, for just three dollars, picked out a really super one. We'll worry about how we will get it home later. At the hotel we received a message from Jacqueline saying she would be round at 6pm so a quick bath for Ellie but she was evidently very hungry, managed to poo on the towel and then became very agitated. It was a real disaster. No sign of the French so don't know what the problem was. The TV news was full of yesterday's bombing; the pictures showed the extent of the damage and we learnt that the number of dead now stood at two. An early night since we both seem to be so tired.

Sunday 11th February

Today, Ellie appears to be very snuffly and I am able to cry off the trip to the lake with no feelings of guilt. After breakfast we slept for another hour. Jacqueline rang mid morning to say that, at last, they have their baby with them. She sounded as concerned about looking after him as I had been when we first had Ellie. It gave my confidence a real boost to realise how far we had actually come since that night. Can it only be less than two weeks ago when Ellie became what I shall always think of as ours? Hence, the reason for yesterday's no-show. I imagined that they were in panic mode. Been there. Got the T-shirt!

We arranged to visit at 3pm and found their hotel easily although the roads were very busy and the noise of the traffic seemingly more horrendous than usual. Jeremy, as he is called, is a very bonny baby, much bigger and far more alert than Ellie with a mass of dark hair – but nowhere near as pretty! He is just nineteen days younger than Ellie. The top of his head has the same trapezoidal shape as hers but more so! I gave Jacqueline one of my bottles with sixty disposable bags which I thought she will find useful. A strange baby present but we've found nothing worth buying for them in the shops at such short notice. We stayed chatting and comparing notes for some time, pleased that they, too, now had the baby they longed for. Jeremy has come from an orphanage just outside Hanoi and had been abandoned at birth by his mother, about whom little was known. We returned to the hotel having collected the passport photos on the way. They had actually turned out very well. Our first baby photo! Ellie had now discovered that her whole fist will fit into her tiny mouth and seems to gain much pleasure from sucking it at bath time. Another day over.

15

Will We Be Expelled?

Monday 12th February
Today is 'E Day' or the day that our visas expired. After today we will no longer be tourists but illegals, not a thought that either of us relish or want to dwell on. We can hardly believe that the five weeks stamped on our visas has disappeared. Of all our original worries this was certainly not one that we had forecast or expected! We saw our first lizard in the bathroom today, a very tiny, dextrous little creature that scooted around at an incredible speed and was really too small to cause us any concern. We named her Lizzie. So original!

Chien came at breakfast time with the paper we had been waiting for from Ha Bac, which we could now produce, if necessary, to the police or immigration authorities to explain that we are in the middle of the adoption process. We have to visit the Immigration office with our passports and hope that they will extend our visas. It all sounds quite simple but will it be effective? (We never did find out exactly what this document said.)

On the way we looked into the Singapore Airlines office where the staff were as friendly and helpful as ever.

We cancelled Wednesday's flight but there appears to be a problem for Saturday as all seats seem to be taken. A mass exodus for Tet probably the cause.

We arrived at the Immigration office at 11am with Ellie in the sling, as usual, but quickly realised that nothing is ever simple in Vietnam and that this is not going to be an exception. No one seems very interested, just a shrug of the shoulders and blank faces. This is, according to them, a big problem. Room 7 eventually sent us to room 6 where we waited for a very long fifteen minutes. Finally, we were sent back to room 7 again only to discover that the window had now closed and everyone appeared to be leaving. We stood there like a couple of lemons whilst the official behind the counter ignored us. John then approached a second clerk behind a desk in the corner who finally explained that we didn't have the correct papers from Ha Bac. Apparently, as we later discovered, this clerk seemed to think that we were applying for a passport. We were made to leave then, having understood nothing of what had gone on and both feeling utterly powerless in the face of such officialdom. Outside I could not stop the tears – the product of frustration, exasperation and sheer terror. This is all going horribly wrong.

Ellie, placid as ever, had remained asleep throughout the entire proceedings. We hurried back to the hotel unsure about what to do next. Madame Director, on reception, could see how terribly upset I was and rang Chien to relay the problem for us. She arranged for us to meet Chien at her office straight after lunch.

Again, we quickly explained the chain of events of the morning and Chien then took us to visit a friend of hers who worked in immigration to ask his advice. We waited outside and she shortly rejoined us with the bad news that, no, a tourist visa could definitely not be extended under any circumstances. Not the news we were hoping to hear. We all went back to the Immigration Office and remained outside whilst Chien went in to do the talking. The answer did not change. It is not possible. All we can do, said Chien, is to push for the ceremony tomorrow and pay by the day for the extra stay.

How that is supposed to work, neither of us could fathom out. The whole thing is an utter mystery and I felt absolutely wretched. Sick to the stomach was a term that I could easily equate to. We returned Chien to her office, via the ice cream parlour where we treated her and, once there, she rang Ha Bac. Maybe the Leaving Ceremony will take place tonight? Who knows? The problem is that we can't get Ellie's passport until the Leaving Ceremony's paperwork has been completed.

A second visit to Singapore Airlines and hurray! Seats for Saturday are available but a bassinet not confirmed. A bassinet is a baby basket that hangs off the bulkhead at the front of each compartment of the plane so that parents don't have to nurse babies throughout the flight. But, who cares! We would willingly stand all the way if necessary! We returned to the hotel via the lake where we again saw Hoa.

Today has been very hot for the first time and so it was a relief to reach the shelter and air conditioning of our room-cum-sanctuary. A shower and a cold beer were sheer luxury and we passed the time with cards and then our meal. We waited and waited but still no news from Chien. Eventually, at 8.15pm, there was a knock on the door and the duty receptionist announced that he had come for our passports which, apparently, had to be taken to the police station. Sick with worry and in a panic I rang Chien who asked that the boy ring her before he left for the station. She said that she hoped the Ceremony would be tomorrow but that she won't know until the morning. This nightmare seems to go on and on.

The passports were taken and we waited anxiously, expecting a knock on the door at any moment and an escort to the airport. My head was pounding and my bowels appeared to have a mind of their own. So easy to lose weight in this country; we are both beginning to look pinched and drawn. I have probably lost about half a stone but John considerably more. The lad returned on his own – Madame Director said there would be no problem for us as within three or four days we would be in England. Oh, how I wish that could be so! It seems hard to believe that Ellie will have no memory of all this. She has slept so soundly throughout this latest panic and I wish that we could say the same. The problem appears to have been sorted out for the moment and we settled down to watch an episode of *MASH* followed by an episode of *Frost* with David Jason. Normality has kicked in yet again – until the next time.

Tuesday 13th February
It was a very good night for Ellie but by 6am I felt really unwell. It turned out that I had a monumental stomach upset, whether due to something that I had eaten or sheer nerves, I had no way of telling. John asked for breakfast to be sent up and I managed some dry bread and tea. At 10.30am the phone rang and Chien told us to be ready for 12.30pm. It looked as though something was about to happen, at last.

John decided that it would be useful to pack away items that we no longer needed and we were able to get one of the large blue-and-white vases we'd bought from the bicycle-pushing peddler into one of the blue box and wedge in with other items. This was one less problem to worry about and gave us a sense of returning home. I washed my hair

129

and decided what to wear. It would have to be the new silk blouse purchased in Hang Gai a few days ago since it was too hot for the one smart jumper I had with me. Chien arrived at 12.45pm and rang Ha Bac again but could not speak to the person she wanted. Never mind, she decided, we will go anyway. This was much better timing for us since it meant Ellie could have her feed and nappy change before we left. 1.15pm and another call came through. 'They' were waiting for the People's Committee to sign the final documents. We must be ready to leave at any time as, if it is not today, it will be tomorrow. Chien left to return to her office explaining that she would ring as soon as there was any news.

It was now 1.25pm and we were all ready. John in the best suit that he had brought all the way from England especially for this one occasion but which now hung off him showing how much weight he had lost; me in the new green blouse with black ski pants and a floral scarf to brighten it up and Ellie bathed and changed into a pink baby gro. The tension in the room was almost tangible but we had no idea how long we must wait.

Finally, by 3.30pm, we had undressed since we were both so hot and were sat on the bed disinterestedly playing cards to pass the time. I rang Chien at her office to see what was happening and, amazingly, she was just about to ring me! The People's Committee were at a meeting 'far away' and so it would not be possible to have the Leaving Ceremony today – but tomorrow instead. Definitely, I ask? Definitely, I am told but I added my own mental 'maybe'! 'Maybe definitely' was a phrase we had coined several days ago but it has become rapidly less amusing.

My stomach seemed to have settled down by now. It was 4pm and so we decided to go on our normal walk for some fresh air and a change of scenery. The pressures of the day had taken their toll and we both felt incredibly despondent and dejected. Nothing seemed to be going our way. As we surmount one obstacle so another appears to take its place. By the time we reached Hang Gai my head had started to ache. We returned to a shop to exchange a T-shirt and by now I felt positively unwell. My head swam and I asked for a chair and sat down with Ellie still strapped into the baby sling on my chest.

The next thing I knew was coming round on the floor with Ellie half lying under me. Water was everywhere since I had knocked a vase of flowers off the counter. In fainting I had fallen forward into the corner of the counter and had managed to cut the bridge of my nose and my cheek under one eye so there was plenty of blood. Luckily Ellie seemed fine although, as the floor was stone, it was amazing that she had suffered no real damage. The shop assistants were wonderful: patched me up and then called for a cyclo. It was Ellie's first time travelling on one but I felt too ill to even think of that. With John dancing worried attendance on me we returned to the hotel where the rest of the evening passed in a blur of semi-consciousness. John put me straight to bed where I lay with a throbbing head and aching neck until, mercifully, I fell asleep – rising briefly at 8pm only to almost keel over again. At 10.30pm I managed to carefully wash the blood off my face, not convinced that I hadn't broken my nose. After that I slept, to wake and give Ellie her 3am feed whilst John did the one at 6am. I didn't think it was possible to feel as low as I did this evening. It seemed to represent the culmination of all our troubles rolled into one and our whole trip seemed to have disaster written all over it.

16

The Leaving Ceremony

Wednesday 14th February
St. Valentine's Day. The first since we were married when
we had not exchanged cards. Maybe there would be an
even greater significance to today. We certainly hoped so.
With Tet only four days away we are now on top a precipice.
If the Leaving Ceremony doesn't take place today we can
see no chance of us leaving for at least another week, if not
longer, by which time John could well have no job to return
to. He has already told me that he must take Saturday's
flight, if necessary on his own, and I may have to complete
the rest of the proceedings alone. This is something that
I don't even want to contemplate. It is bad enough to be here
together. I don't think I would be able to survive physically
or mentally without him and the thought of a long haul
flight home with no assistance is just a nightmare. But, we
will cross that bridge if and when we come to it.

8.30am and a phone call from Chien told us to be ready
for 9.30am. Yes! 'definitely maybe' was 'definitely' after
all! At last! Please God that, this time, all will be okay.
Suddenly, after all the time we've waited, we find ourselves
in a big panic to be ready on time. I found it impossible to

eat much and bathed but left my hair. I had a black eye with a cut underneath, another L-shaped one across the bridge my nose and a sizeable bump on my forehead – although my head has just about stopped throbbing.

By now I had concluded that I had had a belated allergic reaction to the anti-malaria tablets I had taken.

At the appointed time we were downstairs waiting and Chien arrived just 10 minutes late and very surprised by my appearance. She looked very smart and was wearing the brooch we had given her, a small but positive link between us. We took a thirty minute ride in a taxi to Ha Bac and there we met the second go-between again. Then the problems began. We had not realised that the gift of the TV to the family was to be accompanied by a cash donation and, consequently, John had only a small amount of money on him. The situation was looking desperate. Finally, the other woman's husband agreed to lend us some money until tomorrow when we can get to the bank. The alternative would have been for John to return to Hanoi there and then to visit the bank himself. Luckily we were spared this and signed a document promising to repay the loan, taking on trust the wording it contained. We felt relief that this latest problem had been overcome relatively easily and, above all, quickly.

Even now, we still had little idea of what was expected of us, unsure as to whether the 'mistakes' were due to our poor communication or whether the 'rules' were constantly being changed – or being made up as we all went along. We could only agree since argument had proved futile in the past and we were now so close to the final scenes.

With the money arrangements now over we were invited to lunch with the other go-between's family. Ellie took her bottle very well and the daughter then held her so we could eat. We sat on low chairs at a tiny table containing many different and, to us, unusual dishes accompanied by some plain rice. We were too nervous to eat much and the numerous flies buzzing round were not an incentive to partake freely. We were given some mango wine to drink and then two bottles as a gift.

After the meal I went through to the room behind to find the toilet and was amazed to find myself in what had to be the kitchen. It bore no resemblance to anything I had ever seen before for culinary use. There was an open fire raised barely above floor level but nothing that you could describe as a work surface. To create so many different dishes must have been a feat of great enterprise! Beyond this, and to one side, I discovered the toilet, a hole in the floor just like a French camping site and no door or toilet paper. I returned to the 'kitchen' and discovered a small room where I could wash my hands. It contained a shower area but this appeared to be used for washing clothes, whilst opposite was a smart pink basin with running water but no drain connection, only a bucket on the floor under the plug-hole. I returned to the lounge where I changed Ellie whilst the husband disappeared in a taxi to fetch the birth family from their village, Vu Duong.

We waited, still not knowing what timescale we were working to, and eventually left the apartment at 12.45pm. We had thought that the Leaving Ceremony had been arranged for 1pm so either that was wrong or we were going to be late. Apparently, when we asked, it didn't matter. Time was not an issue. Nothing new there, then!

After a twenty-minute drive we arrived in Ha Bac which, we believe, is the principle town in the province of Bac Ninh. We were all shown into what we assumed to be the equivalent of our town hall and then into the building's main hall which seemed to be as run down and filthy as everything else we had encountered. We were ushered to sit at a low table and given the traditional tiny cups with the evil tasting black tea. The cups were, again, very dirty-looking and under the table was a slops bucket for the waste. We were introduced to several men, in particular to two whom, we were told, we should be eternally grateful to since they had arranged everything 'very quickly' and especially for us. I should hate to be here when things go slowly!

Today, we were told, was the last day of Leaving Ceremonies before Tet and we silently breathed a sigh of relief that our luck had finally held. We sat and waited with new worries crowding our thoughts. Would the family come or would they change their minds at the last minute? Neither of us could believe that they could contemplate giving up one of their babies. We knew exactly how we would feel in the same situation and it wasn't something I wanted to dwell on. Two French couples arrived with their babies, the first we knew that the ceremony would not involve only us. Apparently the time had been changed to 3pm but nobody had thought to tell us.

At last, the family arrived and we breathed a sigh of relief: Mum (who we already knew was called Ghi), Dad, his thirteen year old son and Ellie's twin sister, Huyen (pronounced Wyn). Almost immediately there was a sudden splash of water onto the tiled floor as the baby performed a wee. Mother took her outside but I followed and indicated to my nappy bag that I could help. We returned inside and I laid Ellie's twin on my changing mat on top of a wooden bed at the back of the waiting room. I took off the wet sodden triangle of cloth around her middle and put on her first ever nappy.

This was the first time we had seen, in the flesh, this tiny being who was the other half of Ellie and we were keen to compare the girls one with the other. She was so very similar to Ellie but much fatter and longer with skin that appeared to be exceptionally white, like alabaster. During the day we noted many similarities in mannerisms from the way she screwed up her mouth and face to the way she held her head. She also seemed to be more alert than Ellie and took more interest in her surroundings. We laid them side-by-side on the bed for a photo-shoot but Ellie continued doing what she does best, sleeping! We noticed a similar dimple on Huyen as on Ellie at the side of her mouth, but this time to the right rather than the left!

This was also our first meeting with father, a very short and skinny man who seemed to be completely overwhelmed by the entire proceedings. His rather swarthy skin was, presumably, the product of a lifetime of working in the open air. We were told that his name was Son and he was clearly totally overwhelmed by the situation in which he now found himself. He smiled nervously and John immediately went to him and the two men embraced. Each spoke to the other in his own language and with tears in his eyes. They looked a little like father and son since John was head and shoulders the taller.

The 13 year old boy was a good looking lad but spoke no English either and so we had little means of communication. We gave them photos taken of Ellie and some showing our home. Also postcards of Weston-super-Mare showing the beach, the donkeys and other local views – and some baby clothes that we would no longer need. Grandma, in her mid-eighties, had sent her congratulations and her best wishes which, apparently, was deemed to be very good news for us. We had hoped that we might have seen her but this was obviously not to be.

Now that the family was here, our anxieties subsided and I was able to empathise with how they must be feeling. It was a difficult situation for us all and our emotions impossible to put into words.

At last, it was time to move through into the main hall beyond, where two rows of trestle tables were covered in gaudy plastic cloths. On them was a selection of sweets and cans of Fanta which we had previously given Chien money to buy after she had advised us that it would be expected. We couldn't help wondering if the two French couples had also contributed. Many photos were taken with us looking comparatively smart alongside the other couples who were dressed in jeans and T-shirts. However, by now I looked a sorry state with my bruises deepening and we both looked pale and drawn.

A raft of documents were produced which, apparently, had to be signed by all of us. There were six copies of each form and this took a while to organise. Once signing was completed Chien rushed off with one set to the Immigration Office in Ha Bac to start the passport process rolling. She returned relatively quickly and, to our relief, before the actual ceremony itself began since we were relying on her to translate the proceedings for us.

The family presented us with a board inlaid with mother of pearl and inscribed with Happy New Year in English. There was a place to add a calendar and Chien jokingly said that February 14th should be inscribed there. She then moved back into the waiting room and, remembering the calendar on the wall, pulled off the date and gave to us. (We still have it.)

Ellie's birth mother, Ghi, then needed to breast-feed her baby and asked at this point if she might also feed Ellie one last time. This really brought home to me the emotion of the situation. I could hardly refuse what was really her last request, yet it seemed strange to see 'my' baby back with her natural mother in such an intimate way. It did not exactly perturb me but it felt a strange experience and made me realise that, even now, she was still not truly my baby. Ellie, the little traitor, tucked in greedily, as though the last sixteen days had never been.

Eventually, the Minister of Justice for the Bac Ninh province arrived and we were ready to begin the ceremony. He, apart from John, was the only one in a suit, all the other officials being far more informally dressed. He spoke and, after a pause, what he had said was translated into French. We were left rather to our own devices with Chien whispering a rough translation into our ear which John tried to tape on his hand-held tape recorder. We were then formally asked to agree to send an annual report back to the Justice Department to keep them informed about Ellie's well being and progress.

During the entire Ceremony John and Son stood side by side clasping each other's hand and both very clearly extremely moved by the enormity of the occasion. Ghi did not appear to be as moved and I did not see her cry but I felt sure that she was hurting inside. Then, each couple in turn was asked to embrace the other family and we were all given our individual copy of the documents. The adopting fathers were each asked to give a short speech which was then translated with John and Son both becoming exceedingly emotional. John had brought his suit all the way from England for this very moment and spoke movingly. He thanked the Minister for his handling of the Leaving Ceremony and Chien for all her help during the whole process. He thanked the family for the precious gift of their little daughter and promised to keep in touch with them and to send photographs at regular intervals, especially at birthdays. After every phrase, Chien translated what he had said into Vietnamese for the officials and the family. His speech seemed to be well received.

With the formalities over I was able to believe that

Ellie really was now our daughter, a moment tinged with massive sadness as I was so conscious that my happiness was at the cost of the greatest loss for her natural parents.

It was now time for a celebratory Fanta drink with some little biscuits and wrapped sweets.

John gave a handful of sweets to Ellie's half brother to put in his pocket to take home for the other children. We later discovered that he was called Dong and was the father's eldest child, aged fourteen. At last, it was time for the family to leave so we escorted them outside where we had an emotional leave-taking. Both John and Son said a few final words and it was at this point that we made our promise to return when Ellie was eight so she could meet her family and have some understanding of her background and heritage. It seemed appropriate that this would not be a final 'goodbye' for them and that we could, perhaps, give them a lifeline to cling on to and some hope that Ellie would not be forever lost to them. They could already see that she had put on weight and was obviously being well cared for.

The family disappeared in their taxi (no doubt organised by Chien) and we were able to set our sights on the immediate things to be done in order to hasten our departure. We went immediately to the Immigration Office in Ha Bac and waited for forty five minutes while Chien sorted out some documentation. Sitting outside in the car, we watched two dogs scavenging in a basket, one only a puppy. Two men were chatting at the side of the road, both squatting with their feet flat to the ground. To us it looked most uncomfortable but everyone, including quite elderly people, seemed to be able to squat in this way, not sitting on their heels as we might do. We had tried it ourselves in our room but had always fallen over unless we had only our toes on the ground!

It was so hot in the car and we were both starting to feel rather weary- no doubt due to the release from the nervous tension we had experienced up until a short while ago. It was certainly lucky that Chien had dropped off the papers earlier since the clerk had been able to process and complete them. Next stop, the Police Station for another stamp on the documents but, for some reason, it was too late to do this today and we were told that this part of the process would have to be completed tomorrow. More delay. After a quick consultation, it was agreed that Chien would ask the other go-between to collect the papers tomorrow and bring them to the hotel when she came to collect the money we owed her husband. This meant a quick visit back to her house to sort this out and yet another wait in the car.

By now it was 6.30pm and John fed Ellie using one of the cartons of milk we had brought with us for emergency use – and this was it! She had been so good all day, hardly a murmur, and she must have been as hot as we were. Finally we were on our way back to Hanoi passing several bicycles with live pigs strapped to the back. They had obviously failed to attract buyers and were now returning home to live for another day. Or maybe they had been bought and were going to a new home, perhaps to await slaughter.

It was 7.45pm when we walked back into the hotel and I immediately rushed upstairs to bathe and change Ellie.

Chien, who had remained downstairs, eventually joined us and we discussed Ellie's passport. Apparently, it would normally take a week to come through but for one hundred US dollars we could have it on Friday. John wrote out a letter at her dictation giving the reasons why we would need a passport quickly to travel on Saturday, changing it only to improve the quality of her English. Pressure was again put on us to give some extra money to the other woman for all her help. We were rapidly feeling ground down by all the gratitude we were expected to feel to so many people not really knowing whether it was justified or not.

Eventually she left and it was midnight before we went to sleep only to wake for Ellie's feed at 2am and then both being unable to sleep after that. It had been such a traumatic day that the events were crowding round inside my head whilst the immediate future was by no means settled as to when we might finally be able to leave. The start of the shut-down for Tet was now only four days away.

17

Ellie's Passport

Thursday 15th February
At 8am John left for the bank with our money worries mounting since we now had little cash left. Luckily, the hotel would accept my Visa card for their bill. Hopefully, Singapore Airlines will do the same for Ellie's ticket.

Whilst he was gone, Chien rang to say that she would come with her colleague at 11am (not 9am as we had arranged) and that all seemed to be fine for the passport to be ready for Friday. Singapore Airline rang to confirm that they have flights for us on Saturday, so I was able to cancel the back-up date we had in place for Monday. Hurray, things are looking up! Singapore Airlines also confirmed a bassinet for Ellie so everything seems to be falling into place, finally. At 11am Chien arrived alone and more haggling over money took place. She was clearly not pleased that we had less than she had suggested and so I had a quiet word with John resulting in an agreement that he would add in the US100 dollars set aside for the passport and visit the bank yet again tomorrow. This seemed to please her so we hope that now everything else will go smoothly and that there will be no more surprise payments to catch us

New Year's Eve, 1995

First view of the baby, with Chien & Ghi

Family handing over baby Ellie, Vietnam 1996

Baby arrives

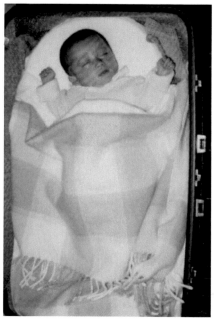

Suitcase bed

Leaving Ceremony, Vietnam 1996

With Liz Levy (left) & Judge Darwell-Smith (right)

First birthday, 1996

Ellie and Grandma, 1998

Ellie's 4th birthday, 1st November 1999

October 2001

Hanoi street scene (note the family of 4 on the motorbike)

Ghi with the twins, Ellie (left) and Huyen, 2004

5 siblings, 2004

Ellie (left) and Huyen with chopsticks, 2004

Huyen (left) and Ellie Playing cards at Ha Long Bay

The new bike – Ellie (left) and Huyen

A tearful parting for Ellie (left) and Huyen

Vu Anh, Vietnam, 2007

Ghi and Son, 2007

Ghi's mother and family with Ellie (left) and Huyen

Ghi and a sister with Ellie (left) and Huyen

Huyen (left) and Ellie at a 2007 mayoral function

Ghi's mother presents Huyen (left) and Ellie with necklaces, 2007

Huyen cooking a rice dish at Elmsleigh Road

Ellie (left) and Huyen off to first day at Sidcot, September 2007

Huyen's (left) first Christmas in England, 2007

The four of us with Ellie (left) and Huyen, August 2010

out. It seems that as long as we are here we are continually being asked to provide money for everything from the car to Ha Bac to the translation of documents. We have, literally, nothing left to spend now so any shopping is completely out of the question. Since it appeared that the other woman was to be late, we arranged to meet Chien at the passport office at 2pm.

We pottered around finding little things to do and were almost ready to leave at 1.10pm when the receptionist rang up to say that we had visitors, the other go-between and her husband. We had no way of understanding them and Anh, the receptionist, tried to translate for us but with little success. At this point Chien rang and, presumably, told them that she now had all of the money. We were able to glean through Anh that they were concerned that we didn't have a clear understanding of the money (how right they were!) and that it is earmarked to be passed on to other people who have been involved in the process. The husband, like John a mathematician, was at pains to show John that he well understood how his mind worked. We assured them that although we had not understood this before from Chien we were now happy and we continued to play down the situation pouring oil on troubled waters in order to bring matters to a close.

The wife volunteered her address and phone number so that we can send items for the family to her and then handed over the letter for the passport office. We were told what else we needed to take and warned not to open the letter. We explained that we were meeting Chien at 2pm and then all was smiles, thank you's and goodbyes. At last, success seemed to be within our grasp and we rushed to complete our preparations arriving, after a hurried walk, at the Passport Office at just before 2pm. Today was very hot and the heat draining. We went to room 6 and waited

143

outside for Chien – and waited and waited.

Eventually, at 2.40pm, we guessed what must have happened. Chien, realising we now had the letter, had either decided that her presence was not required or had told us this on the phone and we had not understood. By now my stomach had turned to water again. Had she let us down? I certainly hoped not! We didn't have her office number and the phones only operated with cards here so we had no choice but to go ahead on our own before we run out of time. Already precious minutes had been wasted.

The clerk on the desk, apparently in army uniform, was the same one who had been so unhelpful on Monday, with not only limited English but also, I suspected, a limited intelligence as well. He was a very large man and his speech was punctuated by long pauses when one wondered whether he had gone off to sleep. His whole demeanour was ponderous to the extent that it was difficult to conclude whether he was considering matters or, worse still, if he was completely ignoring us. Our dilemma now was how much or how little to say. Would it be possible to jeopardise the whole process through a wrong word or whether, by insufficient communication, we might not put our case strongly enough? We selected the middle road and were logged into his book. Things were looking up as he seemed to accept our flight confirmation slip and the covering letter from Ha Bac. All our documents seemed, thank goodness, to be in order and he wrote in his book the date for our collection of the passport.

Peering through the glass screen and reading upside down, John saw, with incredulity, that the clerk had written the date for the passport to be collected as Saturday 24th February. The end of NEXT week! Our flights were booked for Saturday 17th.

'Excuse me, sir,' he said, 'We need to have the passport by this Saturday. Our flight to England is booked for this Saturday afternoon. The 17th. We must have the baby's passport by then.'

The clerk looked at him as if he was mad.

'But I am very busy,' he said.

John's thoughts were probably unprintable. On the evidence before us either of us would normally do more in a couple of hours than this fellow would seem to be capable of doing in a week.

John was on the horns of a dilemma. He had no way of knowing if this was the clerk who had received some or all of the one hundred US dollars we had given Chien to hurry things along but now was not the time to be faint-hearted. The only thing to do was to introduce her name into the conversation. He told the clerk that our friend, Madame Chien, had advised us that it would be possible to have the baby's passport by this weekend.

At this and without a word of reply, the clerk slid sloth-like off his stool and disappeared slowly behind a wooden screen. We had no way of knowing if he was coming back or had finished with us and we stood there like the prover-bial couple of lemons and riddled with worry. Eventually, we asked a female member of staff on the next counter whether our chap was coming back and she went to find out. She returned to tell us that we must continue to wait. We sat down again, mouths dry, hearts racing. Eventually, our clerk returned and clambered back onto his stool.

'You come back Saturday,' he said. 'Maybe passport be ready then.'

'Maybe' was the best we could possibly hope for and, after thanking him profusely (and through somewhat gritted teeth), we accepted a receipt and left. Our levels of stress had just jumped up another couple of notches.

The chances of leaving this Saturday had never appeared so remote, in fact I had little faith that we would be able to leave on ANY Saturday! We walked dejectedly to Chien's office in what was, by now, blistering heat and asked the 'boy' on the desk to ring upstairs for her. Luckily he remembered who we were since we hadn't her extension number with us. Within a few minutes, Chien appeared and we explained the situation to her and gave her the clerk's name which John had copied down: Hoa Manh Cuong, a name we would never forget. It turned out that he was the slow one that she did not like and had been hoping to avoid. No doubt another reason for her not turning up to meet us! We joked and laughed with her over his manner and attitude and Chien was almost in hysterics when John exaggerating his sloth-like movements. We also explained how we had both tried to get our heads through his 'window' at the same time in order to hear him and she was in stitches. It was a relief to feel that, for once, we were all in agreement.

Chien took the receipt explaining that it was not a problem and that she would sort it out although by now I had little faith in anything. All we wanted to do now was collect our photographs and return to the peace, quiet and coolness of our room and, once there, we made a superb shandy with a 7Up and a lager – quite the best drink I had tasted since we arrived.

We rang Jacqueline and related this latest saga to her, even including the details of the Ireland loophole which we had never mentioned before since we did not want them to know too much of our business. At the back of my mind I am worried that any disclosure of such plans and possible loopholes might rebound on us. It was a rotten evening with both of us in very low spirits and feeling incredibly dejected. We had hoped that, at this point, we would have been in a far more positive frame of mind, knowing that the passport was being processed and would be ready tomorrow. However, this was obviously not the case and now our uncertainty seemed to be extending right to the very end. Ellie, thank heavens, has been marvellous all day, no trouble whatsoever, almost as though she has picked up on the atmosphere and realised that the best course of action was total compliance. I slept well out of sheer exhaustion but John could not settle and quietly watched TV during the night.

Friday 16th February

Woke at 7am to the usual sound of cockerels and the noisy hum of traffic. We were up early to feed Ellie, and I succeeded in getting an entire bottle of milk down her front before I realised that the top was cross-threaded, thinking instead how hungry she was! The resulting bath was one she really enjoyed, she finally seemed to be coming to terms with total immersion and even liking it. At 8.30am Chien rang to tell us that the passport would be ready for collection at 8am – tomorrow! Apparently, it hadn't been possible to process it for today since we had not gotten to the passport office yesterday before lunch. It was typical of our luck that this business won't be resolved until the very last moment. It would have given us such piece of mind today to know that we would definitely be leaving tomorrow. Now we must wait yet another day with uncertainty clinging to everything we did. Should we pack in anticipation or would it be bad luck to pre-empt the situation?

We were late down to breakfast and spent time chatting to Anh whose birthday it was. We admired a jade ring she had received as a present and then John who had tried it on as a joke forgot to take it off when we returned upstairs.

I quickly ran back to give it to her in reception and she was in a dither because she did not want her Director to know that it was her birthday. On my return to our room she rang up in a panic since she was worried that the Director might think the ring was a present from us. What strange ideas these people seem to have; everything seems to be such a secret. We planned our day and took another look at our finances (or lack of them!) We decided to stroll to the lake to collect our photographs and to buy Chien a card and a small present for Tet. We really can't afford anything else and it will give us the opportunity for a last 'goodbye' – we hoped – to Hoa.

Back at the hotel we learnt that we had missed Chien who had explained to Anh that we might get the passport tomorrow. What? This was not being couched in terms that gave us any confidence whatsoever. We rang her office in a very worried state but were told that there was no problem after all and we could relax. We arranged to meet Chien the following morning at the airline office after we had – hopefully – collected the passport. Shortly after, Jacqueline rang to say she would be round on her own since it was too hot to venture out with her baby, Jeremy. We passed a pleasant hour chatting and looking at her photographs. We discussed our different situations, the money we had spent and the time everything had taken for both couples. There are Danes in her hotel who are able to adopt through an agency which is so much easier and involves a stay of just two to three weeks. After she left at 3.45pm we felt like a change of scenery. John has prepared himself and, stemming from our precarious financial position, persist-ent beggars and cyclo boys are no match for him! We saw Hoa again and spent some time chatting about her family who farm rice in the countryside. She showed us a picture on one of her postcards of a man ploughing a paddy field with an ox apparently just like her father did. John used his hand-held dictaphone to tape her chatting with her friends which made them all screech with laughter when it was replayed! A final (we hoped) goodbye and then we returned to pack in a half-hearted manner, first the second blue box and then I made a start on the baby bag. Another phone call from Chien to say she was coming round and our stomachs churn yet again. What can be wrong now? As our food arrived in our room so did she but it appeared that there were no problems except that the passport would, apparently, be ready at 9am not 8am.

Another lost hour we could ill afford and the stress continues. We arranged to hand over the 100 dollars passport fee at the airline office and later reflected that it seems strange not to have given it to her tonight unless it was some sort of safeguard in case the passport was not ready. More cause for concern for our over-active imaginations. We chatted amiably making small talk whilst she explained that she was off to the countryside tomorrow to visit her family for Tet – for the entire week so it was certainly lucky that we are due to leave this weekend or we would be totally stuck without her. Finally, she left and we attacked our packing with more confidence than we had felt for a long time. Ellie, as usual, had been as good as gold. Goodness knows how we would have coped with a difficult baby in this situation. A last gin and tonic, a game of rummy and an increasing feeling of optimism clung to us. Please don't let us be counting our chickens prematurely!

Saturday 17th February
Ellie had a reasonable night although she did not take her bottle well. I feel sure that the tension surrounding us must have been more than obvious to her. John barely slept all

night, tossing and turning with worry and breakfast was a sad affair with neither of us able to eat without feeling sick. This really is the end of the road for us and if the passport is not there we will have some serious decisions to make. We were ready far too early and so passed the time playing cards trying to focus our minds on something other than the immediate future. We decided to use our limited funds on a cyclo rather than rush to get there on foot, our first offer of 6000 dong was refused but the second cyclo driver accepted and we meandered through the streets via a tortuous one-way system.

We approached the desk with trepidation. It seemed as though the culmination of all our efforts was being captured in this one moment and that success or failure would now be decided. We were told to wait whilst a lady clerk went to check. She returned shortly afterwards and told us that we must wait five minutes. This was definitely looking promising since we had not been sent packing which we had been afraid might happen. Finally, at 9.05am, a second official came out of a door from behind the counter – and she was smiling! The very first smile we had seen from any official in more than four weeks and certainly the first we had seen in this dour building. And in her hand was an envelope. And in the envelope was Ellie's passport.

We were overcome with relief and I was ready to burst into tears as I felt the tension drain away. I do not think I actually realised how wound up I had been until that point of physical release. More form filling and lots of smiles from everyone, I was so happy I could have forgiven anyone, even Hoa Mang Cuong…

Well, perhaps not!

18

Up, Up and Away

We were now on a mission to beat the clock and left the passport office on foot. We must have looked a strange sight to the locals as we ran through the streets and were both perspiring profusely by the time we arrived at the Singapore Airlines office. Chien had arrived before us and after sorting out the tickets and paying by Visa we bade her a restrained goodbye. I handed over the biscuits and card for Tet whilst John queried the money already paid before handing over the final US100 dollars for the passport. It was all rather embarrassing and I was anxious to leave. Chien was smartly dressed and had only gone into the office to say goodbye to us since she was off to her province at lunchtime. We fully realised that we could not have managed without her but there was a lurking belief in both our minds that the whole process had taken so much longer than it might have done and that it had been in many people's interests that we should have been detained in Hanoi for much longer than might have been necessary.

The meeting and goodbyes over, we hurried back to the hotel via the lake for one last time. The postcard sellers had all returned home for Tet so there was no-one to hassle us and no Hoa to say a final, final goodbye to. It seemed really strange to be leaving at last and doing everything for the last time. It was as if life had taken on a new meaning and I could look at the scenery through different eyes. We had done it and we were, at last, going home as a family!

Back at the hotel it was 10.20am and we rang Jacqueline and Anton to tell them the news, John gave an almighty 'whoop' down the phone and we said our goodbyes. We were both hot and sweaty from our exertions so were glad of a cool bath. John reckoned that we had loads of time to pack but I knew differently and when the taxi came at noon we were still not quite ready and needed another ten minutes to finish. A final goodbye to Anh on reception and we were off. This time I am so excited that I can hardly believe it is happening and that we really are leaving at long last. John took some photographs from the taxi windows of this final journey, our 'passage to freedom', as we passed the army officials at the toll booth part way to the airport. I can easily imagine how escapees must have felt leaving behind their previous lives. The sense of release was overwhelming.

On arrival at the airport we encountered a problem with the taxi driver who demanded thirty US dollars. The taxi had been arranged by Chien who had told us that the fare would be twenty US dollars and we simply did not have any more cash on us. John pulled his pockets inside out to show we had no more money and the driver eventually shrugged and drove off. We decided that he had just been trying it on.

The task of checking in went relatively smoothly and we breathed a sigh of relief. John had decided to book all our luggage through to London instead of Dublin. He certainly could not afford the time to travel to Ireland and back if he was to return to work at the very earliest opportunity. If necessary I would have to travel alone. I sincerely hoped that that would not be necessary. We were then able to move through into the Departure lounge where we had to offer our passports to the two uniformed guards on the gate. One of them scrutinised the documents carefully and then exclaimed 'But your visas are out-of-date!'

What could they possibly do to us now, we wondered? At best a fine, money we did not have. At worst, perhaps they would detain us even longer but that did not seem a likely or logical alternative. Since the whole point was that we should not be here I could not imagine that keeping us even longer would be a sensible solution to the problem. John tried to explain that we had been involved in a drawn-out adoption process and produced the document from Ha Bac. It was a considerable relief when these officials eventually waved us through – but not before we had to find a final few thousand dongs as an exit fee we had previously known nothing about.

John

Reading Anne's diary so long after the event I cringe when I am reminded what a wimp I became as time wore on. I had always imagined that pure bloody-mindedness would enable me to survive being chained to a radiator in downtown Beirut like Terry Waite or John McCarthy but I failed a much gentler ordeal quite miserably. How I admire Terry and John and others like them. Their fortitude – sustained by their faith – was, and is, truly awesome.

In my defence, I have always done the planning in our marriage and Anne had always been content to leave such things to me. The fact that everything was completely out of our hands was hugely frustrating and, of course, the pending expiration of our visas was a constant worry since we knew that an extension was completely out of the question. We were, therefore, faced with the prospect of being deported at any time after February 12th – two days before the eventual Leaving Ceremony and a full five days before we actually left. If that had happened, we would have had to say goodbye to Ellie.

I was also extremely worried about my job. Of the sixty students on my law course, only around twenty five percent of us had obtained training contracts. Although the partners at my firm had beaten my training salary down to a fraction of what the Law Society recommended, I desperately needed to hang on to the position if I was to complete the practical side of my training. Messages that were coming from the senior partner, via my sister, were extremely worrying and I was anxious to get home as soon as possible.

With hindsight, we should have come home after dealing with the initial paperwork and then gone back to Vietnam a month or so later for the Leaving Ceremony and to bring Ellie home. However, we soon found that we had a tiger by the tail and letting go did not seem to be an option when we were constantly expecting the Ceremony to be just around the corner.

I was also dealing with money matters and had completely miscalculated the amount we had needed to take with us given that our stay was turning out to be so much longer than we had anticipated. These were the days before credit cards were so readily acceptable in Vietnam and we had at our disposal only a finite amount of money. I felt very much like a driver with a rapidly emptying tank wondering and worrying if he was going to make it to the next petrol station or not.

These were pressures and frustrations made so much worse by the fact that we did not dare to leave the hotel for more than a few hours at a time in case the next stage in the

154

process was sprung upon us without warning. We would have loved to explore outside the city, to go away for a few days to see some of this historic, beautiful and interesting country but we did not dare to. Neither could either of us indulge in a favourite pastime of reading. Newspapers and books in English were non-existent and television was the only distraction – although rather repetitive.

However, as Anne describes, after the row with Chien I was, at last, able to adopt a more philosophical (fatalistic, perhaps) attitude to the whole situation and felt the better for it. We both worried, of course, although Anne, as usual, tending to keep hers to herself rather than to articulate them to me. In some ways, our 'ordeal' was a huge distraction but, on reflection, did it make the whole experience much more special and sharp in our memory?

I rather think that it did.

19

Homeward Bound

Anne
That surely must have been the last hurdle, at least as far as
leaving Vietnam was concerned. Time later to ponder on
any problems that might occur at Singapore. We eventually boarded the flight out of Hanoi on the first of the two
legs of our homeward journey and were shown to seats in
the centre of the plane. My emotions were very mixed. On
the one hand, I was euphoric to be leaving at last but, at the
same time, I could empathise with the feelings of Ellie's
family as we were taking her thousands of miles away. But,
not forever, because we had vowed to return but they were
not to know whether those were empty promises or not.

At last we were airborne and able to relax. Our flight
was one of the last out of Hanoi before the whole country
virtually closed down for the week of Tet, the Vietnamese
New Year. John joked that he would have sat on the wing,
if necessary, to get to the relative security of Singapore.
Potential problems still lay ahead but, for a few hours at
least, we could enjoy the moments as the plane ate up the
miles on the first stage of our homeward journey.

Our seats were located just behind one of the serving

stations and, after take-off, cabin staff brought us a bassinet (a kind of carrycot) which was clipped onto the bulkhead in front of me. This meant that we both had the opportunity to rest and Ellie was relatively quiet.

Eventually, we landed at Changi airport, Singapore, where we had a wait of around five hours for the London flight. Ellie remained her usual placid self and spent a lot of time sleeping in the baby sling. John and I also tried to get some sleep but had little success and, of course, the closer we got to departure time the more concerned I became about Ellie's lack of a visa. There were many shops to wander around although a slightly pointless exercise when your purse is empty! At one point I realised that my period, not due for another two weeks, had started and I had to spend precious cash on some tampons since mine were all in my luggage. It seemed to prove how upset my body rhythms had become during the whole saga. Something else to make me feel unwell in my run-down condition.

John rang Gill and Rod (reversing the charges) to let them know that we were on our way home, the number of our flight and our anticipated time of arrival at Heathrow. They immediately confirmed that they would be there to meet us.

At last the time approached for our flight to London and so we slowly moved to the departure gate which was on the second floor. A long queue had formed leading up to a glass door through into the departure lounge. This was manned by airline staff who were examining the tickets of the passengers as they passed through.

With my heart in my mouth we slowly edged forward. Just act naturally, said John, there shouldn't be a problem. Act naturally! How could I possibly do that whilst I continued to fear the very worst? Just because the tickets to Eire had worked for Sue Loveday, who was to say they would work for us? What if the rules had change, what if, oh, a thousand different things?

Our turn next and I felt desperately sick. John handed over our three passports.

'And the baby's visa?' queried the official.

John produced the onward Heathrow-Dublin plane tickets for the three of us and explained that we were flying on to Dublin where children under sixteen did not require a visa. The official was obviously aware of this and, with that, we were waved through. It had actually worked!

Thank you, thank you, THANK YOU, Sue Loveday!

We boarded. London and 'normality' one step closer. Surely now we are safe and can finally relax. Surely 'they' cannot refuse us entry into our own country and how could they return a defenceless baby, legally ours, back to a country where she belongs to no-one?

As we settled into our allotted seats, John noticed that some of the passengers immediately in front of us were talking over the heads of other passengers to two other people sitting in the front row of our section about five rows away and immediately in front of the bulkhead. He approached the two and asked if they would like to swop seats with us so that they would be sitting closer to their travel companions. They readily agreed and we immediately relocate to their seats. As soon as we were airborne cabin staff produced a bassinet for Ellie and for a much more comfortable journey for us.

During the flight, Saturday 17th became Sunday 18th.

I had been so anxious about everything else to do with this journey that I had really given little thought as to how I would cope with a young baby. But Ellie was certainly the least of my problems and made a difficult situation far easier than it might have been. We tried to sleep through the long night journey but with little success. The air conditioning made the aircraft cold and it was a struggle to keep warm even though staff produced blankets for us. As we moved closer to London our thoughts turned to the reception that might be awaiting us. Another unknown, another worry to be surmounted. We were so looking forward to seeing Gill and Rod again and had so much to tell.

John

On our flight back to Heathrow we comforted ourselves with the knowledge that we had tickets for an onward flight to Dublin if the absence of a visa for Ellie proved an insurmountable barrier to direct entry to the UK. I had surmised that if we then took a flight from Dublin back to Bristol International Airport we would not be subject to the same immigration controls as we would if coming in from a non EU country. Alternately, we could come back to Weston by train or car without being subject, I assumed, to the same entry scrutiny as we were now facing on our return to London direct from Vietnam. It sounded alright in theory but we had left England for a three-week stay and here we were returning nearly five weeks later. Anne was still very unwell and worried about the Corn Dollies' ability to keep the wholesalers happy. I was concerned that the rather unsympathetic senior partner at my firm would not take kindly to my overstaying my leave by such a big margin (he had already made somewhat threatening noises to my sister on more than one occasion when she had telephoned him to explain our extended stay) and it was important that we got home as quickly as possible. We concluded that we did not really have time to go on to Dublin, as planned.

We landed at 6am on a cold mid-February morning – such a difference from the sticky, humid atmosphere we

159

had left behind in Hanoi. I had arranged for our luggage to be off-loaded at Heathrow and once we had collected it from the carousel we presented ourselves at immigration. And what a sight we must have looked! Anne with two black eyes and a large, slowly-healing cut across the bridge of her nose and me, having lost one and a half stones, with my clothes seemingly hanging off me.

We queued with the other British passport holders to pass through the immigration gate, not quite sure what else to do. The next few minutes were going to be vitally important and when it came to our turn I explained to the immigration officer how it was that we had no visa for Ellie: how the adoption procedure had taken so much longer than we had anticipated so that our visas had expired making it impossible to apply to London for a visa for the baby to be processed and sent out to us in the diplomatic bag (a process that would have taken around three weeks according to British embassy staff in Hanoi); the fact that we had consequently planned to fly on to Dublin and apply for a visa from there; Anne's ill-health and accident and the prospect of my job no longer being available unless we could go straight home. The officer heard me out and then directed us about twenty yards away to the head of a long queue of Hong Kong Chinese waiting for their entries to the UK to be processed.

This was a real eye-opener for us and showed how stringent the checks are on foreigners seeking to enter the UK legally. Standing just a few feet away from the nearest desk we could clearly hear the line of questioning being directed at each of them. Where were they intending to stay? How much cash did they have with them? How had they come by it? What was the length and purpose of their visit? The questions continued relentlessly until the officials were convinced of the genuineness of the replies.

Whilst we waited I picked up a form from a nearby table and completed it with all our various details before we were eventually called forward by a young Bangladeshi woman sitting behind a tall desk that reminded me of the teachers' desks during my time at Weston Grammar School for Boys all those years ago. We were both very conscious of how we must have looked

She examined our passports and I repeated the explanation that I had already outlined to the previous officer to explain the absence of a visa for the baby; I again emphasised how we had been delayed in Vietnam and could not wait long enough for a visa to be issued from London which would have taken another three weeks, at least; how the Singapore Airlines official at Changi had allowed us onto the London flight only on sight of our tickets to Dublin from where we had planned to make Ellie's visa application; how Anne's accident and sickness from the anti-malaria tablets and my potential job-loss made it imperative for us to get home as soon as possible. She took our passports and disappeared into another room, presumably to consult with her superiors, before returning to tell me that she would issue Ellie with a temporary twelve-month visa – after which we would then have to apply for an extension whilst we were involved in the UK judicial system of adoption.

We were through but then, as a parting shot, she called after us to say that Singapore Airlines would, most probably, be fined for bringing us in! Of course, I immediately repeated that the Airline's staff at Changi had done nothing wrong and had only allowed us onto the London flight on sight of the onward tickets to Dublin. The official shrugged as if to say that that was the way the system works. It is to deter airlines from bringing passengers to the UK with no right of entry. I made a mental note to write to Singapore

Airlines as soon as I got home.

We passed through the Green channel and out onto the Arrivals concourse where Gill and Rod were waiting for us at the barrier both beaming in welcome and hardly able to wait for their first glimpse of the baby. Our reunion was very emotional and then Rod went off to fetch the car.

Shortly afterwards we were homeward bound along the M4 motorway swapping our stories with their up-dates of local news and their take on my firm's attitude to my continuing employment. They dropped us off at our house with an invitation to lunch at theirs and left us to unpack.

A couple of hours later and after a refreshing shower we drove the six hundred yards to Gill's home – only to be surprised by the presence Anne's mother, Doris, her brother, Ian, his wife, Marion, and Gill's two daughters, Rachael and Claire.

The baby was much admired!

And so we settled into our new life. No longer just the two of us but a family of three. I went back to work the next day and it was evident that my training contract would continue as before although I was deemed to have had my entire holiday entitlement for the whole year – and part of the following year, too! I had no alternative but to agree and the partners, with long memories, kept to that decision and a number of days were deducted from my holiday entitlement for 1997. Nice people!

Within a day or two I had written to Singapore Airlines to explain that their employee at Singapore had acted quite properly in allowing us to board the London flight on the evidence of our Dublin tickets as presented to him.

The airline replied that they had already been fined £2,000 – which was considerably more than our combined fares. Outraged, I wrote back asking who I should write to in order to have this injustice overturned and was pleased to be told, a week or two later, that the fine had been refunded – but thanks for the offer.

20

Adoption in England

John

I had also written to Social Services to advise them that we had completed Ellie's adoption in Vietnam and that we were now about to apply for an Adoption Order in the Weston-super-Mare County Court. Although I had been studying law for over two years I had no knowledge of adoption procedures but it was fortunate that my niece, Claire, worked in the Bristol County Court office and was able to provide me with the required application forms and helpful guidance about the process generally.

We had completed Ellie's adoption in Vietnam fully in compliance with the laws of that country. The process had been completed at the Leaving Ceremony presided over by the provincial Minister of Justice when all the final documentation had been signed by all parties: the Minister, Son, Ghi, Anne, and me. It was only at that point that we had the necessary paperwork to enable us to obtain a passport for Ellie and leave Hanoi as a family.

However, that was not good enough or sufficient for the powers-that-be (PTB) at home. We had brought a child into the country without a visa and without approval. We had been well-aware of this from the outset and were ready to face the consequences, if necessary. But we reasoned with each other that we had the PTB over the proverbial barrel. Whatever they might be empowered to do to Anne and me they could hardly take Ellie away from us. To return her to Vietnam? To take her into care? We were convinced that neither was a realistic option.

Nevertheless, it was a worrying time.

The matter was listed in the Bristol County Court rather than Weston-super-Mare because of the availability of more senior judges and given to Her Honour Judge Susan Darwell-Smith. At the first hearing her whole demeanour indicated that she was not impressed by what we had done. A former social worker, Liz Levy, was appointed as Guardian ad Litem to look after Ellie's interests and a firm of Bristol solicitors appointed to act for her. I decided to represent Anne and me myself – mindful of, but despite the old adage that a lawyer who represents himself has a fool as a client.

The central issue revolved around whether Ellie's birth mother, Ghi, had given her consent to the adoption. I argued that the final adoption papers, which we had all signed at the Leaving Ceremony, were proof enough that Ghi's consent had been given. After all, there had been six original copies signed by all parties and one given to each of us to retain. I produced one of our copies. But no, this was not good enough for the Courts of England and Wales. A Consent to Adoption form had to be completed. Nothing else would do!

The Judge ordered that a translation be prepared and sent to Vietnam for Ghi's signature to be obtained and witnessed. But how to get it to her? This was the Court's dilemma and I decided to let them get on with it. Posting the form to Vu Du'o'ng was not an option since Ghi's

165

signature had to be witnessed. I explained, innocently and truthfully, that we had never visited the village and did not know exactly where it was. No, I could not think of any way the document could reach the village. Perhaps the British Embassy could help?

At subsequent hearings we heard that the Embassy did not have anyone to send out into the sticks for the purpose. Surprise, surprise! Then the Red Cross was mooted – and other possible agencies but none turned out to be practical. Anne and I waited and waited for the due process to exhaust itself. Time dragged on. 1996 evolved into 1997 and the Home Office extended Ellie's temporary visa for a further twelve-month period. We were summonsed to attend further hearings at Bristol County Court but no progress was made.

On one occasion one of my clients had a divorce and children's matter timetabled for the same morning as one of our own hearings. When our matter finished there was a general change of personnel in the courtroom as Anne left to go home and I moved further back to sit behind the barrister I had engaged to represent my client.

Now, no-one but the parties and their legal representatives are permitted in court for family matters and, peering over her reading glasses, Judge Darwell-Smith enquired of my barrister, "Who is that man sitting behind counsel?"

Of course, she knew full-well who I was but presumably thought that I had stayed behind to watch the next proceedings. I could not help seeing the funny side of the situation as my barrister, after looking over his shoulder to see who the Judge was referring to, with obvious puzzlement explained that I was his instructing solicitor! Ignorant of the previous proceedings, he must have wondered whatever the Judge was on about!

I think that, in the end, we simply ground the Judge

down. She had done her best to follow procedure but there was no way she was going to obtain Ghi's witnessed signature on the Consent to Adoption form. She eventually fell back on my original suggestion that Ghi's signature on all the adoption papers executed at the Leaving Ceremony would suffice.

Another hearing was listed for 30th October 1997 – nineteen months after the original Application had been made – and Liz Levy, very supportive throughout, indicated that she thought that the Order might be made at that time. So we took Ellie with us. Judge Darwell-Smith emerged from her Chambers wreathed in smiles and, to our absolute delight and relief, proceeded to make the Adoption Order.

She then invited us into her Chambers where she made a fuss of the baby before arranging for photographs to be taken of the three of us with herself and Liz Levy. Unfortunately, our camera jammed after just one snap!

Ellie celebrated her second birthday two days later.

21

Ellie's Development: 1996 – 2004

Anne

Life was strange in those first weeks and months after we returned from Vietnam. John had slipped easily back into his old routines and embraced the joy that Ellie was giving us. The reality, I found, was somewhat different and I envied the piece of mind that he had so readily achieved. For me, it was as if those weeks in Hanoi had left a permanent scar that I knew would take a long time to fade. It was as if my focus on a world I had been so familiar with had shifted slightly and now my vision was blurred. Everything was the same, yet all was different. I was constantly aware of that parallel world that was Vietnam, thousands of miles away, where life was as far removed from ours as it would have been on another planet. It hovered at the back of my mind with a lingering sense of depression that I found difficult to shake off. Perhaps this was my own personal version of 'baby blues' for surely my body had been through as much (and more) as anyone who had carried a child for nine months and then given birth.

The immediate problems I faced were huge. Before we left I had no time to make long term plans for life on our return or dared to predict an event so tenuous in the making. Superstition and bad luck all entered the equation and I guessed it would all sort itself out, as-and-when. Well now, here I was and I was the one who had to sort it all out as well as care for a new baby. Six weeks of orders, wages and unpaid bills from the business had to be dealt with and the staff, who had stepped in and coped so gallantly, were ready for a well-deserved rest from all their recent additional duties. I also had to pick up my 1/10th Physical Education timetable at Worle School (abandoned back in January at such short notice) which meant child-care was required every Friday afternoon. The staff, my 'Corn Dollies', were wonderful and new rotas were quickly made leaving me working afternoons only when I was able to take Ellie into the shop with me. I was proud to show her off to the customers who were all so interested in what had happened and I was pleased to repeat the story which became a type of catharsis, helping me to dispel the shadows of the past. Ellie had her own special place in a basket placed in the shop window where John especially loved to put her on a Saturday morning when he was working with me. He would visibly swell with pride as people noticed her and commented on how cute she looked.

Ellie fitted seamlessly into our everyday life and was quickly accepted by all, even our two Abyssinian cats! As with so many childless couples they had been 'our babies' and basked in all of our affection whilst receiving 100% of our attention. Despite a certain 'coolness' towards her at first they soon realised that this tiny scrap was here to stay. My initial reservations of any jealousies they might harbour were completely unfounded and I soon trusted them implicitly around her. In turn they became part of Ellie's everyday life and she learnt to treat them with love and respect whilst they, in turn, learnt to put up with some initial tail pulling!

Once the practicalities of being home were arranged I was able to revel in the experience of being a new mum. People were so kind and genuinely interested in our story and Ellie. Presents and cards poured in for many months as friends and little known acquaintances heard our news and wished to welcome Ellie into the family. Such love and consideration was, for us, overwhelming and would never be forgotten. Life became not just a new chapter but almost a completely new book itself, certainly one with a new cover! It became a series of firsts – starting with Mothering Sunday two weeks after we returned. Previously and BE (before Ellie) this had been a day of some sadness for me, each one tinged with a 'maybe next year'. Well, now it was next year and finally I could also be one of the gang, my heart bursting with the same pride that thousands of mothers before me would have experienced in their new babies. And, with no shadow of a doubt, Ellie was a brilliant baby!

Four weeks after we returned she slept right through the night. I remember creeping into her room each morning full of fear to check that no disaster had occurred in the night. Each morning, John and I would vie with each other to see who would be the first to pick her up and bring her back to our bed for a cuddle, the separation of the night seeming a lifetime. I was so lucky in that Ellie, being small, loved to sleep and we quickly established a routine together where it was not unusual for her to sleep for four hours in the morning, giving me much needed time for paperwork, housework and gardening. This, unbelievably, continued right up to three years of age, only stopping when she began playschool.

During this time the UK adoption process slowly

lumbered on like a sloth with, at times, no perceptible progress. We had contacted social services on our return informing them of Ellie's presence in the country and had received the first of many inevitable visits. I had no real concerns that the adoption order would not be made eventually but I was aware that it might be unwise to holiday abroad until all was complete since Ellie only had her Vietnamese passport. An unnecessary worry, I am sure, but I felt that it might be tempting fate if we went out of the country before Ellie had a British passport.

Social Services came to call. My major concern was whether John would be able to toe the line and manage to keep his temper as we answered relentless questions about our religion, family life and even our sex life. Provisions were also made to interview family and friends to find out their views on our suitability as parents. Such a shame that natural parents are not subjected to the same rigorous testing. It might even lower the number of children in care!

But, eventually, Ellie's adoption order was granted a few days before her second birthday and we were able to breathe a sigh of relief as she was finally acknowledged by the powers-that-be to be lawfully ours. Such a marvellous day and one we recorded by placing an announcement in both our local papers and the *Exmouth Journal* at my mother's request.

I was aware every day what a precious gift a child is and what a privilege it was to have Ellie. It was an amazing thing to be in the position where you could shape someone's life and I felt sure that nurture shared an equal place with nature in the grand scheme of things. I was determined to do the best that I could for Ellie and she was given the care and attention that can only be given to a first child.

We attended clinic regularly each week where her slow weight gain was a source of great concern. The percentile charts we were following were meaningless and there didn't appear to be any for Asian children. Ellie's slight anaemia also gave cause for concern and she was quickly tested for thalassaemia, a genetic blood disorder prevalent amongst Asian and black communities. We spent a worrying two weeks waiting for the results which were then, thankfully, negative. At first there were so many tests, some repeating ones done previously in Hanoi as well as new ones such as checking for TB immunity. The blood was always taken from the vein in her tiny hand, impossible for some nurses to find at the first attempt. This would cause such anguish for us as well as for her!

Slowly, she began to thrive and our worries for her health diminished as we learnt to appreciate that she would develop at her own pace and comparisons with other children were pointless and unnecessary. She was, by the textbook, always slow to achieve the milestones of development such as sitting, crawling and walking but within two years had made up for her slow start in life. She was a bright and perceptive child and quickly became a constant source of joy to us both. A whole new world opened up for me and I was keen for Ellie to have as much contact as possible with other children. She and I began attending weekly mother-and-baby sessions at the nearby village of Hutton and I soon became involved in the running of the group and continued to do so for the next two and a half years.

Next, at the age of three, came playgroup and I was unwise enough to volunteer for the post of treasurer – soon coming to realise that it was almost a full time job! Luckily, this corresponded with the point in March 1998 when we finally decided to close the shop and I had more free time to concentrate on other things. The business was making huge demands on the time we now wished to spend with

Ellie. This coupled with the fact that the health food trade was undergoing a radical change with regard to the potential licensing of supplements and the increasing competition from supermarkets made closing a wise proposition.

At some stage, Ellie's transition from cot to bed had presented her with the opportunity to come into our bedroom in the morning if she had woken early. She would try to haul herself up onto the bed by clutching and pulling on handfuls of duvet – aided by one of John's hands under her nappy. Happily snuggling down between the two of us she would usually drop off to sleep again but, when that did not happen, John would usually tell her a fairy story. One day, for a change, he made up story about a little puppy he called Bob. After that, Ellie would always come into bed with the request, "Tell me a Bob story" – and a whole collection of Bob's adventures came into being. There must have been around fifteen of these entirely original stories and I was just as keen to hear how they would unfold as Ellie was. Bob thwarted robbers and animal snatchers; on a family holiday to America he went up in a rocket instead of the monkey; he followed his friend, John, to school and created mayhem; he rushed onto the pitch and ran the ball into the goalmouth when he should have just been watching John play – and usually managed to get his photograph in the local newspaper after some heroic deed or other. John admitted to me that he had no idea how each story would unfold from one sentence to the next and that he was just as surprised and entertained by them as Ellie was! Perhaps he will get them published one day if he can find an illustrator.

And so our lives entered another phase where, for the first time in twenty years, our weekends were free to plan as we wished. This, eighteen months before Ellie started school, was a time of great enjoyment for me. I continued to be as busy as always, still doing some supply teaching when possible but without the added pressure of the business and the staffing headaches that brought. No longer did a phone call at 7.30 am mean rearranging the rota and, perhaps, filling in myself. I was now able to extend my involvement in Ellie's activities which I saw as a way of putting something back into the community. Whilst Ellie was in the Rainbows (the junior branch of Brownies) I stayed to help each week and similarly when she moved up to Brownies. It seemed something of a small thank you to the people who give up hours of their time to entertain and teach our children life skills but unfortunately few mums seem to see it that way. Likewise, I volunteered to be a governor at Ellie's primary school, a post I was to hold and enjoy for six years.

Our life with Ellie has been full and varied. As an only child we are conscious that it would be easy to spoil her but since both of us came from backgrounds where we had been brought up to appreciate the value of money, we would hope not to have done so. We have enjoyed as a family such pleasures as walking, cooking, gardening and making our own entertainments rather than visiting the expensive theme parks that some families favour. Each birthday has always been celebrated in a traditional way with a homemade cake and our large house has lent itself to a variety of party games. I like to think that Ellie's parties have been special because of their difference to the norm and her friends have clearly enjoyed that difference. Grandma presented Ellie with a year book and I faithfully chronicled the first five years of her life in great detail, something, I suspect, I could not have kept up for a second child.

Every so often that book comes out and we leaf through it reminding ourselves of things we never thought we would ever forget: the way she used to love dancing to music, the way she never crawled but suddenly one day stood up in the middle of the kitchen, her tea parties with her favourite toys and the way she always referred to John and me as 'you two'! So many, many memories that now I am so glad I recorded them for posterity. And of course, Winnie, a soft Winnie-the-Pooh toy given to Ellie at eighteen months by John's cousin's wife, Rosie. Never could a toy be more real not just to Ellie but to all of us. He is included in all our daily lives in fact, when Grandma knitted Ellie a new scarf , a little one was included in the parcel as a surprise for Winnie, too!

As in many families, we have our own 'rituals' as well. The yearly birthday photo taken on the same step of the staircase wearing the party outfit, the only change being the year we used the wrong step and the change of carpet and décor; the mixing of the Christmas cake with the wish, never to be disclosed or it will not happen and the advent booklets to be placed on a small artificial tree in her bedroom counting down the days to Christmas. These are the things that I will always cherish because they represent 'us', our family and no one else.

My mother's relationship with Ellie has always been a constant source of pleasure to me and far better than I could ever have hoped. She was, at first, called Da Da by a tiny Ellie and they have spent many hours playing together, mum with a patience and understanding that I doubt I could emulate. The juxtaposition of the young and old together and mum's love for her new granddaughter has brought a warmth to my heart, not least because it so very nearly didn't happen. We see her as often as possible but the sadness is that because I was a late baby for Mum and I was so late having Ellie, Mum's days with her will be numbered. This, I know, is a fact of life and cannot be changed so I must be grateful for her continued good health with her advancing age.

Ellie has turned into a delightful child with a distinct personality of her own. She has a marked sense of right and wrong and as she rarely oversteps the boundaries herself, is incensed when others do so. If, as a family, we are doing something she considers 'not allowed' she remains troubled until we stop or it is put right. She can be a stubborn child and cannot bear criticism, knowing her own mind on most things. This makes for many arguments when she and John lock horns, both trying to get across their point of view. She is also an extremely loving child and enjoys close physical contact with us both. She is generous with her money and especially her sweets (far more than I am, if the truth be known!). She is fascinating company and has a delightful sense of humour although, unfortunately, this rarely translates to being able to take a joke against herself. She has never been able to cope with people laughing at her, even as a young child and this can lead to a sulky reaction which others fail to understand. Her temper can easily be lost and she is quick to rise to John's merciless teasing, not yet being able to shrug it off.

She loves family life and is happiest when we are all together at home. This has made it difficult for her to spend time away from us and in many ways she is a shy child which can make her appear sullen to people on first meeting. She has been brought up knowing from the very first that she has not only a whole family in Vietnam but also a twin sister. Hopefully, our openness with her has given her an acceptance of the situation and we have encouraged her to think about them, to talk about them, even what they might be doing at certain times of the day and to take an interest in Vietnam as a country. She has a notice board beside her bed full of family photos, both

176

Vietnamese and English. She often speaks of missing Huyen although I think this is more to do with the idea of having another child to play with than the fact that she is her sister.

Ellie loves to be around other children and sometimes finds it lonely at holiday times and weekends. Because of this we have always gone out of our way to encourage other children to visit and, occasionally, sleep over. Ellie does not always find it easy to make friends and sometimes feels she is different to the others in her class. I'm not sure where it stems from but hope it is more to do with her shyness than any sense of her nationality or her situation. She is a competitive child as, from experience, most children are and, as a family, we enjoy competing with each other whether at cards or in some silly made-up game.

Ellie's progress intellectually has been excellent and whilst we were aware that any child we adopted might not have our own intellectual capacities, it has been refreshing to see Ellie's keenness to learn and the abilities she has shown. We have, hopefully, been able to make learning fun for her, even down to the games we play on car journeys such as the 'alphabet' game where, in turn, we must come up with a word for each letter of the alphabet for a given category such as animals, towns or countries. This, in particular, has been a great favourite with her that we have passed on to many others. She has developed a tremendous love of reading which I like to think is, in part, due to the amount of time I have spent reading to her at bedtimes. This especially pleases us because not only is it a vital learning tool but also a marvellous and self-entertaining thing to be involved in. I like nothing better than to be in the middle of a good book that I can't put down and I know Ellie often feels the same.

We have tried to instil in Ellie an understanding of

politeness and good manners, increasingly difficult in a world where, it seems, little value is placed on such things. She knows that for every present received either at Christmas, birthday or any other time she must produce a written thank-you note, which she is very good at doing. Initially, I would do these on her behalf so it is now one less task for me! We also feel that it is important for families to continue to do things together and to spend time talking to each other. For us, this is at mealtimes when we always sit down to eat together for every meal at the kitchen table. In the evening this has developed into a time when we each give an account of our day, starting with the oldest. Ellie now refuses to discuss her day with me on the way home from school making me wait until she can tell us both together.

The demons of our time in Vietnam did eventually disappear but it was probably some eighteen months before I felt truly back to normal and in tune with my surroundings again. I can see how much I have learnt from Ellie and how I have grown and changed in that time. She has made me think about my own beliefs and ideas and is always questioning, wanting to know why. She has taught me how easy it is to love another human being and that the act of birth is only a very small part of the whole process giving no credence to my now distant fears that I might not be able to love her.

Above all, I have learnt that love means the unselfishness of being able to put another person before yourself.

22

Correspondence 1996 – 2004

John

In 1996, the principal adopters in Vietnam were, and maybe still are, Americans, Swedes and French. They were all assisted by adoption agencies in their own countries which would deal with all the necessary arrangements and the adopters were only required to go out to Vietnam for a few days to complete various paperwork at some early stage in the procedure and then to return a few weeks later once their child's leaving ceremony had been arranged.

Antoine and Jacqueline Saavedra were the exception to this arrangement and were ploughing their own furrow. How they sustained themselves for around two months, I shall never know. Clearly they were far more resilient than I was and, apparently, had far more supportive and understanding employers. They were the only other couple we met who were adopting without agency support. In fact, until we met the French couple who shared Ellie's Leaving Ceremony we did not encounter anyone else who was adopting. We did see one or two small coach parties but these appeared to be tourists. In all our time in Hanoi we did not come across any other Brits.

Anne and I convinced ourselves that if Ellie had gone to America, Sweden or France she might never have known of her birth family let alone that she had a twin sister still in Vietnam.

The promise I had made in my speech at the Leaving Ceremony had not been given lightly. Anne and I were determined to keep Ellie and Huyen in touch with one another until such time that they would be able to maintain that contact themselves. How that might eventually be we had no clear idea but we had the comforting thought that the twins might possibly be reunited one day if that was what they both eventually wanted for themselves. At best, we imagined that that would happen when they were eighteen or older.

I began writing to Son (Tran Dac Son, Ellie's father) two or three times a year with a simple progress report and photographs – the letters being translated by Cuong Cao before they left Weston. Cuong also translated the replies which arrived with the occasional photograph of the family and the developing Huyen. The photographs were clearly taken professionally and, we later discovered, by a photographer who had a small studio on the outskirts of the village. They were always laminated and I wondered if this was a tradition to protect photographs from the local humidity.

During the run-up to the 1997 General Election I had become very friendly with Margaret Daly, the Conservative candidate for the Weston-super-Mare constituency. Margaret was, and is, a very friendly and colourful character and we hit it off immediately. She also took a keen interest in Ellie. Unfortunately, despite fighting a vigorous campaign organised by her husband, Ken, Margaret was unsuccessful in defending the seat and it was, perhaps, inevitable that her strong European credentials (which

I did not share) should soon see her forging a new career in the EU organisation.

A few months later and out of the blue we received a telephone call from Margaret. She was about to visit Hanoi as leader of a European Community delegation talking to the Vietnamese about different forms of democratic government. Did we have anything for the family we would like her to take with her?

Anne hastily put together one of our by-now-famous blue boxes full of clothes for the whole family, toys, crayons, pens *et cetera* for the children. We also asked Margaret if she would try to open a bank account in Hanoi for Son so that we could transfer periodic sums of money from our account in the UK to his. We gave her some American dollars for the purpose. Lastly, I wrote to Son to tell him when Margaret would be in Hanoi and where she would be staying.

Vietnam had a comparatively new parliament and Margaret's group was there to help identify ways in which the Vietnamese might develop a more democratic form of government; how reforms of the Vietnamese National Assembly's communication capacity might be achieved and how public participation could be enhanced. She talked to politicians and encouraged them to speak independently. She also met with women's groups since, in a recent election, 16% of the female population had been expected to vote and an impressive 26% had actually done so.

Despite this busy schedule, Margaret, on her return, was able to tell us that everything had gone according to plan. Son had arrived at her hotel on the pillion of a motorcycle taxi and photographs were duly taken. He had brought presents – a carved wooden fisherman for Margaret, a twelve-inch high carved wooden Buddha for Anne and me and four wall plaques for Ellie, inlaid with mother-of-pearl. We were very touched but hoped that these had not been too expensive.

Margaret also brought us the name and office address of the Vietnamese woman, Vu Anh, who had translated for her during her stay. She had told Anh our story and our plan to return to Vietnam when Ellie was old enough and Anh had indicated her willingness to help when the time came. I immediately wrote to introduce myself and received a quick reply confirming what Margaret had said.

The bank account now enabled us to help the family in a more practical and tangible way. I would arrange a bank-to-bank transfer of, say, $US500 and then write to Son to let him know that the money was on its way and would soon be available to him. We made a point of trying to do this to coincide each year with the twins' birthday, 1st November.

Son would sometimes write back telling us what they had used the money for. The first purchase was a free-standing electric fan –which impressed Huong Cao when she read the letter her husband had translated for us. Up to that point she had been very dismissive of Son's attitude especially when he asked for money. But for the family not to have previously had a fan was a clear indication to Huong how poor they really were.

Yet Son did ask for some strange things. On more than one occasion he asked us to buy him a motorbike but we felt that this would be far too expensive for Son in fuel and maintenance. He also asked for leather jackets for the older children which seemed to be an odd request in the circumstances. We decided to continue drip-feeding money to him so that the family did not come into large sums – relatively speaking – at any one time which they might have difficulty coping with.

We were also worried that Son might be having to give

money to local officials or others who might be wanting to share his 'luck'. We were totally ignorant of the local hierarchy and what demands might be made of him. We decided to act on the side of caution and I even tried to make any references to money somewhat cryptic in case they were read by others. This was a particular concern when Son asked us to send letters to be translated in the village rather than continue the established practice of having Cuong write his translation between my (English) lines.

We were pleased to hear that Son had bought a cow which not only helped him plough his paddy field but also had the potential to produce the periodic calf that could eventually be sold to increase the family's income. He also bought or rented some additional land and planted potatoes – although a very wet season did not produce much of a crop in the first season.

(We didn't discover until much later that they had been able, with our help, to rebuild their house, setting it back further on the same plot and possibly enlarging it at the same time).

After two or three years we received a letter from Son together with an English translation. It appeared that someone in the village – possibly a new member of staff at the school – had a sufficient command of English to deal with the translation process from their end. The translations were adequate and I think that Cuong Cao was rather pleased to be relieved of the task!

Around that time Anne was introduced by Huong Cao to the Tuong family: Hien, and his wife, Hanh, newly arrived in Weston from Bristol with their son, Hieu, and daughter, Thao, just four months older than Ellie. Hanh was, and is, a very bubbly and friendly person and she and Anne quickly formed a close friendship and Ellie had a new little friend to play with in Thao. When letters from Son began to arrive untranslated again it was Hanh who kindly agreed to help out and my letters were double-spaced so she could write between the lines. In those letters I would try, principally, to give the family news of Ellie's progress and, at the same time, to enquire about Huyen's. We were careful not to dwell too much on the 'treats' Ellie was given and her lifestyle since the comparison with Huyen's would be invidious. For the same reason we were careful with the photographs we chose to send.

Of course, Anne and I were both interested in comparing the two girls. After all, Ellie at 1.2kg at birth (and the younger by two minutes) had initially been two thirds of Huyen's birth weight of 1.8kg. We marvelled at the fact that Ellie had been only six pounds at three months! Huyen had also been originally longer than Ellie by about two centimetres. Yet, within a relatively short space of time, Ellie was heavier and longer than Huyen. Nature or nurture?

It was interesting to note that both babies seemed to sleep well but both proved difficult to feed. Ellie, in particular, would doze off shortly after starting a bottle and had to be 'joggled' to stay awake.

I also told the family a little about what we had been doing and, given the Vietnamese respect for the older generation, a health report on Anne's mother, Doris, Ellie's doting new grandmother. Thereafter Son would always enquire after her. I have a keen interest in family history and tried to elicit a 'tree' from Son to show Ellie in the future. However, the Vietnamese seem to record and have an interest in dates of death rather than birth and the information received was a little disappointing from that point of view.

23

Ghi's Letter

John

The vast majority of letters from the family were from Son, written with a good hand on paper possibly taken from an exercise book but carrying little real news. Vietnamese seems to be quite a "flowery" language and two or three words of English would sometimes be translated as a whole sentence. Son would spend a good part of each letter wishing us health and happiness and often asking for money. After discussing the matter, Anne and I decided to maintain the financial help by continuing to drip-feed money in the same way we had in the past.

We had also received just one or two letters from Ghi in the seven years 1996-2003. She expressed her gratitude that we had adopted Ellie and although she missed her she was so pleased that Ellie was enjoying a much better life in England than she would have in Vietnam.

Then, in April 2004, and out-of-the-blue, came another letter from Ghi saying how unhappy she was; how she was accorded no respect by the rest of the family; how Son and her step children all treated her like a servant and no-one helped her with the household chores. She even threw doubt on whether Son had properly divorced his first wife.

She said that the money we were sending was being spent on the other children and, in particular, Dong, the eldest, was staying out late at night and gambling. On the other hand, all Huyen was getting was the odd exercise book. She begged us to send no more money but to spend it on Ellie instead.

But we were stunned when the letter went on to ask us to adopt Huyen as well – to improve the child's life and so that she, Ghi, could escape her unhappy situation.

As soon as Hanh had translated the letter, Anne and I were absolutely dumb-struck. We decided to contemplate quietly the letter's implications and not to discuss it until we had individually and separately marshalled our thoughts. A day or two later we sat down to compare our conclusions which, unsurprisingly, were virtually identical.

On the one hand we were thrilled at the prospect of achieving our heart's desire – reuniting the twins so much earlier than we had ever imagined. On the other hand we were conscious of the fact that Ghi's letter was borne out of her unhappiness and, possibly, her depression. There was no way we could even consider adopting Huyen in such circumstances.

We also had the dilemma of deciding how to reply to Ghi's letter. We surmised that she had written without Son's knowledge. Presumably, any reply from us would be read by him and we had no idea how he might react towards her.

I made a speculative enquiry of Social Services to see what their attitude would be if Ghi's request was sustained in further letters. I wondered if they would recognise us as a special case with Ellie already adopted and the girls being twins. They confirmed that, in all probability, this would make no difference. As before, the full procedure including a home study would have to be followed if we were to apply to adopt Huyen.

It was also a fact that the British government had tightened the procedure for adoptions from abroad. There had been two high-profile cases in the news: one where a UK couple had actually purchased twin babies from America over the internet (and, I believe, had eventually been forced to return them) and, secondly, another couple who had been caught trying to smuggle a gypsy child out of Romania. The adverse publicity generated by these stories had a lot to do with the government's reaction and I believe that many genuine adopters had their plans scuppered as a result. Such irresponsible behaviour was a tremendous disservice to all those children waiting to be adopted and to the potential parents wanting to do so.

We then received a second letter from Ghi asking us to ignore her previous letter which had been written, she said, when she was annoyed with Son. In reality he was a good husband. The letter was accompanied by two other short letters – one from her mother and one from her older brother. Both said that Ghi had been silly to write. That everything was really OK.

In some respects, this second letter made things worse. It seemed possible that Ghi had written it under a degree of duress. But what to do?

For Ghi's sake, we felt that we had to be very careful in our reply. We were also aware that our letter would have to be translated with precise meanings and nuances possibly being lost in the translation. The best way forward would be by face-to-face discussions with a competent translator in attendance and our thoughts turned to the return visit we had promised ourselves and the family. We had provisionally aimed to go back when Ellie was around eight and a half – judging that she would then be old enough to understand what she was seeing and appreciate the way of life of the Vietnamese in general and the family in particular.

I had written to Margaret Daly's friend and translator, Vu Anh, in Hanoi telling her of our plans to revisit and she readily agreed to help in any way possible. Her English was excellent and we knew that we had the ideal person to accurately and fully explore Ghi's real situation and attitude to her present life. Instead of investigating Huyen's adoption, maybe we could switch from funding the whole family, open a bank account in Ghi's name and, perhaps, she and Huyen could then 'escape' to a new life somewhere else, if that would be appropriate.

I therefore replied to Ghi as if from Anne and as cryptically as possible. I thanked her for her letters and told her that I (as Anne) was looking forward to speaking to her, mother-to-mother, on her own without 'the men' being present so that we could compare notes about each other and the twins.

I suggested that she and Huyen might like to go on holiday with us for a few days. I had long wanted to visit Ha Long Bay, declared a UNESCO World Heritage site in 1994 with over sixteen hundred mountain tops rising out of the sea, that had dramatically featured in the closing scenes of the 1997 James Bond film, "Tomorrow Never Dies" starring Pierce Brosnan. The Vietnamese often tout this spectacular feature, located just off the coast in the South China Sea, as the Eighth Wonder of the World and our plan was to hire a junk for a couple of days and nights and tour this unique and awe-inspiring region. Ha Long Bay is not only considered by many to be one of the natural wonders of the world but is also a symbol of Vietnam and a paradise for photographers.

Ghi replied that she would like to go on holiday but

that she thought that Huyen would want her father to go, too. We wondered if this comment arose out of further pressure on Ghi but felt sure that a woman-to-woman session could easily be arranged whilst I occupied Son elsewhere on the boat.

And then I had a brainwave!

24

Huyen to the UK?

John
Anne and I had spent almost all our working lives in schools and were increasingly dismayed at falling standards of pupil behaviour and achievement. We worried that Ellie, being small and 'different', might encounter difficulties and be unhappy in the hurly-burly of one of the large local comprehensive schools and our thoughts had turned to the alternatives.

Neighbours' children were travelling to Bristol by coach every day to attend two of the previously grant-maintained schools. We were aware of their reputations for academic excellence – indeed, I had taught for five years at Bristol Cathedral School and Mark had spent five happy and successful years there immediately after I had moved on to Backwell – but the travelling added an extra two hours to the school day and so we started to look nearer home.

Sidcot School, a comparatively small private school about ten miles away and run on Quaker principles, had an excellent reputation enhanced in no small way by a large intake of pupils from abroad, especially from places like

190

Hong Kong and China. The three of us went to an Open Evening and were very impressed. Ellie was immediately keen on the idea that she might be joining Sidcot in Year 7.

Could we afford two sets of fees if Son and Ghi were willing to let Huyen come to England for her secondary education?

My retirement years were never going to be 'normal' with such a young daughter to provide for. There would be no cruises, no holidays at the drop of a hat at any time of year. What the hell! Let's go for it!

We broached the subject in a subsequent letter and Son replied indicating that it was something that they would think about.

From our point of view, the proposal seemed to offer the best of both worlds. The twins would be together again years earlier than we had ever dared hoped; we would act as Huyen's guardians in the UK and she would have the benefit of a western-style education.

Also, we had noticed, back in 1996, that some Vietnamese children seem to leave home at quite a young age – girls to sell postcards and boys to act as shoeshine boys to tourists in the city and to live in dormitories whilst sending money back to their families. We reasoned that Huyen would be able to return home during the main school holiday as frequently as she wanted – although only when-and-if we could afford the air fare! Of course, if it happened, Huyen would come to England with virtually no English. Perhaps she might be able to get some tuition in her village although that seemed unlikely. Nevertheless, children learn quickly and we were encouraged by the annual stories in the press of children who had come to the UK without a command of the English language and were off to university a couple of years later with fantastic GCSE achievements behind them. We calculated that if we were

191

to collect Huyen around Easter 2007 she would have some five months before a September start at Sidcot.

I would take a belated and second retirement to be home with her all day and every day whilst Anne and Ellie were at work and school and we would have Hanh and her family close at hand to help with translations, if and when necessary. Although, as a foreigner, Huyen would not be able to attend an English state school officially we harboured the hope that Ellie's primary school Head Teacher might allow Huyen to attend unofficially with Ellie from time to time.

It sounded feasible in theory. Once at Sidcot, Huyen would be able to benefit from a special department run for those children for whom English is a second language.

We put together an information pack to take with us to Vietnam including a copy of the Sidcot brochure showing many aspects of the school including the indoor swimming pool and the sports hall.

John

The next few months saw our holiday arrangements being put into place. We planned to spend ten days based in Hanoi before flying on to Australia for a four-week, four-location stay visiting friends and distant relatives. Everyone but us seemed to be on email and so correspondence with Vu Anh and the Dream 2 hotel in Hanoi and most of our Australian contacts was through the good offices of my sister, Gill. We determined to haul ourselves into the 21st century when the trip was over.

Singapore Airlines generously agreed to my request for additional luggage allowance so that we could take with us items for the village school in Vu Duong. In fact, they doubled the normal allowance for three people and many friends and colleagues rallied round to provide new and good second hand items. Mick Finch, who worked for the local Hospice, gave us dozens of children's items donated by the public but which would not have sold in the charity's shops.

So, visas were applied for, flights booked and accommodation reserved in Hanoi and in Australia. Finally, everything was in place and Anne's brother, Ian, kindly agreed to drive us to Heathrow in our car, minus the front passenger seat as before. Here we go again. To a certain extent, into the unknown as far as Huyen was concerned because Anne and I had the nagging doubt that even if her parents agreed, when push came to shove in three years time, would the child be able to leave her parents and come back to England with us? But at least, this time, we would be in charge of our own destiny. We had a timetable fully mapped out for almost two weeks in Vietnam followed by four in Australia. We were off into the wide blue beyond for our second visit to the other side of the world. Last time we were two. Now we are three.

And, as they used to say in the cinema, this is where we came in.

25

The 2004 Visit – Anne's Diary

Tuesday 20th July 2004

As our taxi entered Hanoi, we began to see some immediate differences. Far fewer bicycles now, replaced by motorbikes in their thousands and even new red-and-yellow single-decker buses, a big surprise! We could not approach the Dream 2 hotel by car since its narrow road had been pedestrianised although motorbikes, we noticed, still continued to use this narrow thoroughfare. It was pouring with rain as we struggled into the hotel with our luggage and immediately noticed changes from our previous stay. The reception desk had been moved to the front of the lobby, the bar removed altogether and the area around the foot of the staircase opened up to include the small dining area which included the manager's computer. A large, plate-glass front door added a modern feel to the entrance. Cuong, the manager, appeared to speak good English although we were later to find that appearances were still deceptive in this country. The good news was that our room had been reserved, the bad news that it was not immediately available and we would have to stay one night in another hotel close by. We took one suitcase with immediate necessities and struggled in the rain and intense humidity to the Bodega Hotel, 5 minutes walk away. Our room there was huge and basic but at least the air conditioning worked and the fan, too. The bathroom was adequate if none too clean but joy of joys, soft loo paper had reached this corner of Vietnam!

We decided not to go to bed but to try to get into the 'Hanoi cycle' as soon as possible by delaying sleep until early evening so, after a quick wash, we ventured out to see old haunts, immediately struck by many changes. We walked up Hang Gai past the silk shops to the lake – noticing that we were no longer out of the ordinary to the Vietnamese since foreigners were evident everywhere. Generally couples, many of them clearly of retirement age and probably Australian, backpackers but few children, if any. Several local people looked at Ellie and then at us with obvious curiosity when they realised she was Vietnamese but we were no longer constantly bothered to buy things as we had been before. The whole experience was immediately so much more relaxing than before. The street noise seemed quieter to us now, perhaps helped by the buses ferrying more people or maybe we had simply become more used to it. At the lake we did not see one card seller and were not pestered at all. A pleasant experience. A student who wished to practise her English joined us and was able to help us buy a street map for 5,000 dong, about 20p. We located the shop where we used to buy ice cream and introduced Ellie to her first, made with coconut milk and a definite winner! The changes in the shops were enormous with so many Western goods available to buy. Many shops had modern display windows and fittings whilst Western dummies displayed clothing in a rather congruous manner. The juxtaposition of old and new seemed even more bizarre now. A twenty-first century shop with security guard on the door might be sited next to a twentieth if not a nineteenth century one where the family were crouched around and eating in their lounge area whilst selling a few items from the 'front room' which opened onto the street.

Around the lake, formal paving and planting gave an added classiness to the city centre and we noted that many buildings had been painted and generally spruced up, too. Finally, we used the guide book to seek out a European venue for our much longed-for meal, amazed at the incredible choice now available. We only had American dollars but our first and closest choice, The Kangaroo Café, would only accept Vietnamese dong and so we eventually located Pepperoni's Pizzeria. An inspired decision, inexpensive, tasty and somewhere we will return to often. By now we were shattered and returned to our hotel to put the light out at 7-45pm, waking only briefly at 1am and 8am until we finally surfaced three hours later after 15 hours of much needed sleep!

Wednesday 21st July

We were soon installed in Dream 2 and at first were given a room at the front which we quickly changed for our 'old' room at the back – larger, quieter and, of course, nostalgic! No changes here except a smaller TV and no satellite but all very familiar. We settled in and looked forward to meeting Anh, Margaret Daly's interpreter of six or seven years ago, who would be taking us to Vu Duong village for our first ever visit and where we would, at last, meet Ellie's birth family and see how they live.

Ellie was given a camp bed and we rearranged the room as best we could to fit it in. Anh, our interpreter, rang and we arranged to see her at 5.30pm. She certainly sounded easy to understand with a good command of English.

Time for more sightseeing so we went off to see the site of the old 'Hanoi Hilton' prison, demolished behind an original and forbidding high stone wall when we had last seen it in 1996. The site is now a shopping mall and offices with only a small section of original wall left. We were intrigued to note that the sign denoting the headroom over the entrance to the underground car park was in English. Another sign of Western influence and a shrinking world. The British Embassy, previously the scene of many anxious moments for us, was no longer in the same, easily recognisable building. We would find its new location later. Cafes were everywhere and we stopped for a drink. Again, the menu was also in English. The rain continued incessantly and had barely paused since our arrival yesterday. We took Ellie to visit the market which she instantly hated, the smells as strong as ever and more dead dogs to view – all part of her 'education'. In Hang Bai, John espied a shop selling delicious looking gateaux and we bought some to eat outside. Only 1$ each and worth every cent! Across the road a new building was, we realised, a department store which stretched across an entire block. We entered and were instantly struck by the efficiency of the air conditioning (in fact, it was, if anything, too cold!), a real bonus after the tropical heat and damp outside. We were amazed to find the store reaching up six floors with two scenic lifts and probably the first escalators in Hanoi. We watched as Vietnamese shoppers (or were they simply inquisitive visitors like us?) struggled to cope with the techniques of using them, fearful first at stepping on then followed by panic to get the timing right to leave again at the top. It was truly a novelty for them all, young and old alike, and must certainly have been on the 'places to visit' list. The store comprised of what appeared to be shops within a shop, each unit, I suspected, renting its own space. On the ground floor perfumes, jewellery, watches, shoes and handbags as well as electrical goods and even a car. It took us some time to work out the prices in millions of dong and certainly they were exorbitant even by our standards. For the Vietnamese they must have been out of this world.

The whole of the 4th floor was given over to a super-market which was entered through turnstile gates manned by a security guard. There were so many Western things to buy from Whiskas to Ernst and Gallo wine. It was a real treasure trove but still no baked beans! Here, to our surprise, most things were much cheaper than at home. The European palette was certainly catered for now. We returned to the hotel to meet Anh who was a real delight, so friendly and positive, a real boost to our spirits. She was a short, stocky woman apparently in her late forties or early fifties, with a face that lit up when she smiled.

She would arrange a taxi and we agreed to leave for the village at 8am the next morning so we could return before 5.30pm since, after that time, the driver would require extra payment. For our evening meal we settled for safety and returned to the Pizzeria but managing to get soaked on our return as the heavens opened up. Slight nerves of anticipation were now beginning to surface with thoughts of tomorrow looming, a day which promised to be a very tiring and emotional one.

Thursday 22nd July

We were up at 7am to give us time to shower and wash our hair but all feeling rather tired – no doubt still slightly jet-lagged. A good breakfast of rolls and fried eggs was appreciated although none of us felt especially hungry. Anh arrived at 8am followed shortly by the taxi. We loaded in only a few things feeling that it would be better to take the presents the next day rather than appearing to arrive as Father Christmas with piles of gifts. The car quickly steamed up in the heat and Anh supplied a constant source of chat and interest which gave us something else to concentrate on.

We soon came to realise that neither Anh nor the driver knew exactly where Vu Duong was, just the general direction. Once we crossed the Red River and cleared Hanoi we found ourselves on a wide dual-carriage 'motorway' with paddy fields on either side and where traffic was relatively light and largely made up of buses, lorries and the occasional motorbike. This was a toll road and John and I were quietly amused to note that our driver had to pull in to the side of the road to buy a ticket from two women covered up against the rain – only to hand it in again at the toll booth just a further hundred yards down the road! Eventually we left this road onto a lesser road and, as before, the paddy fields kept us company along the way. Isolated building sites dotted the route although no-one seemed to be working. We stopped for directions on two occasions and received mixed instructions – on one occasion being sent back the way we had just come! No-one seemed to have heard of Vu Duong and we later discovered that it was better known by the name of its weekly market.

Finally, after one last enquiry, we rattled about two miles down a makeshift track across the paddy fields, hardly any wider than our eight-seater people-carrier and came to the outskirts of a village. Suddenly, through the pouring rain I spied a forlorn-looking couple standing beside a shop under a ramshackled awning and realised it was Son and Huyen. We quickly pulled over and they squeezed in with Huyen sitting on my lap and Son next to me. The time was now just after 9am and it turned out that they had been waiting since 7.30am so they could lead us to the house. Their thoughts whilst waiting for us for all that time must truly have been amazing and since we had had no contact with them for some weeks before leaving England they must surely have been concerned that we were not going to show up.

It was a very, very emotional moment. Huyen seemed so incredibly light and bony sitting on my lap, so like Ellie and yet so different. The two of them kept glancing surreptitiously at each other out of the corners of their eyes, wanting to look but not wanting to be seen to be doing so. John and I both had tears in our eyes, overcome with the emotion of the moment. Now that we had a guide in the form of Son we were able to negotiate the narrow streets through the village once we had turned off the 'main' road. We bumped along tracks full of deep, rainwater-filled potholes and found ourselves viewed with considerable interest by those villagers who were out and about their business. Was it the car? – surely a rare occasion in the village – but we also wondered if everyone knew that we were coming and, certainly, there were some women who were standing by their gateways and might have been waiting for us to pass. We began to feel like royalty and waved through the window at everyone we saw, John one side and me the other. Everyone looked very friendly and waved back. Since our letters had only ever been addressed to the family at Vu Duong (rather than to a particular road), we had expected a very tiny village with just a small collection of houses. However, it took us a surprising amount of time through increasingly narrowing streets to reach the family home, driving down to a river and turning right to follow its course along the edge of yet another paddy field and bumping past many graves dotted along the water's edge. Another right turn into an alleyway between brick walls and only inches wider than our vehicle which we expected would be damaged at any moment if it came into contact with a wall. However, the driver skilfully negotiated this final hurdle and was then directed to park on a neighbour's 'forecourt'.

We had arrived!

John and I were then issued with Wellington boots and, with him carrying an umbrella-wielding Ellie on his shoulders, we all squelched on foot through the incessant rain following Son and Huyen the forty or so yards to the family home – where a host of people were crowded in the doorway and in the windows to see us arrive. Again, having no real sense of the size of the village we wondered who all these people were until Anh later explained that they were all relatives. There must have been over forty of them, including many young children who were all running around in a state of high excitement. It was a real welcoming committee and, again, we felt like royalty – but so BIG! Gulliver (this time with his wife) amongst the Lilliputians came instantly to mind!

As we approached, an incredible number of people tumbled out of a large house across the verandah and down the steps. It was so overwhelming and also very emotional. Ghi was not present as she had gone to the market but there were many aunts, uncles and cousins including both grandmothers, with much laughing and crying from everyone. Everyone seemed to want a piece of Ellie and contact with us!

Son was suddenly conspicuous by his absence, his place being taken by two older men who Anh introduced as his brothers. We slowly realised that there was a very clear hierarchy in operation and the older of the two brothers – as head of the family – was now in charge. During much hand-shaking and hand-holding this man ushered us to a low, blue-tiled coffee table around which were set half-a-dozen very small, low, almost child-sized, plastic chairs – very similar to those that parents of Junior School children will be familiar with at parents' evenings in England. Whilst trying to concentrate on Anh's translation of what was being said to us and asking her to reply on our behalf, we were slowly able to take in the room we were in that seemed to take up almost all of the building.

Although, perhaps, high enough to be two storied, it was open to the decorated rafters and was, no doubt, built in this fashion to combat the periodic high humidity. The entrance double doors were set in the centre of the front wall and there was a barred, glassless window on either side of them. On the back wall two other glassless and barred apertures looked out onto a rear garden area and at the far, left-hand end of the room was an curtain-covered doorway into another, much smaller room. On the wall opposite the front door stood a bulky chest of drawers which seemed to double up as an alter with a photograph of the twins' dead grandfather on the wall behind. Against this back wall, in either corner and under the windows, stood a low, wooden platform about five feet square and clearly beds. We wondered where everyone slept: Son, Ghi, grandmother, Huyen and the three teenagers, a girl and two boys. Surely there must be other beds somewhere else?

Anh was wonderful at interpreting giving time for the answers to be given. We asked about the children and a shy Nam, now 16 was pushed forward. We were next introduced to Phuong who had tears streaming down her face and who could not wait to hug Ellie. It was heart-wrenching to see. Next we saw Dong sitting next to Phuong, a very good-looking 'boy' of 22 and we were amazed to see how emotional he was, too, as he clasped Ellie with very red-rimmed eyes. Suddenly Ghi came hurrying in. We were told that she had been to the market and I should think she had heard of our arrival from the whole village. She rushed over to Ellie and was very, very emotional as she scooped her up, poor Ellie looking totally embarrassed by the whole thing. Poor Ellie! She has never liked being the centre of attraction and despite our efforts to prepare her for these moments she was having difficulty coping with the situation. Additionally, as she has always been small she has often found herself being picked up by bigger girls at school and grown to hate it. Now, here she was being picked up by a stream of complete strangers. Smiling or trying to look pleased was out of the question! Both John and I lost count of the number of times we muttered "Smile, Ellie" without success.

As we sat at the little table, everyone else either stood or sat on one of the two bed-platforms. John took a few photographs of the assembled throng and everyone seemed to be pleased to have their photograph taken – especially the children. We were given homemade wine, strong like a brandy and the older of Son's brothers made a long speech: how happy they were that we had come, how honoured that we had kept our promise to return with Ellie and how much they appreciated the financial help we had given them over the past eight years. There was huge applause from the forty or so relatives now inside the house and I replied saying that we promised to return when Ellie was eight and have done so; how happy we were to see the girls together and how special we found their welcome. There was more applause and toasts before, eventually, things became a little quieter giving us the opportunity to gaze around and take in a little more detail of our surroundings. Behind us was a picture frame full of photographs of Ellie sent by us through the years. On a pillar in the centre of the room was the large picture of Ellie we had sent in 2003 now mounted with a red border above a similar sized one of grandma, now 89! In the other corner was a TV mounted on a cabinet on which also stood a wooden carving, about two feet high, of what looked like a Chinese warrior astride a rearing horse and spearing down on some invisible victim. To the right of this was the open doorway into the far end of the house.

Later we were shown this second room which turned out to house a grain silo for the twice-yearly harvest, a third bed and a desk for the children to sit at to do their homework. We now discovered that Phong shared this bed with her ancient grandmother with the two boys sharing one of the beds in the main room and Huyen sharing the third bed with her parents. John and I guessed that this arrangement precluded further additions to the family!

At about 11.30am, food was brought in by Ghi and several of the other women and placed in four different areas for the different family groups; the low table for the senior family members including us as guests, the two bed-platforms and the floor where everyone crouched to eat and sat back on their haunches. Luckily they realised that this would not do for us; there is no way John or I could have maintained such a posture – whereby every-one adopted a position with feet flat to the floor and bottom hovering a few inches off the ground – for even a few seconds. It was truly a feast by any standards with a variety of interesting dishes including a sticky rice cake normally reserved as a treat for New Year but made especially for us today. We felt a pang of guilt that maybe this feast had put a severe strain on everyone's budget but the occasion was clearly one of great rejoicing for all members of the extended family and we were determined to show our appreciation.

The food was tasty but without the flavours that one

might have expected or normally associate with Asian food and was certainly not spicy. I knew immediately that Ellie would struggle with such a diet and people were most concerned when she ate virtually nothing. A spoon was even offered to her although John and I persevered with chopsticks. Both her uncles picked out choice pieces of meat for her but she would not be tempted – despite John and I hissing 'Just give it a try, Ellie' on several occasions! Huyen tucked in with relish, clearly well-used to everything on offer. A delicious water melon followed and then the girls were each presented with a gift, a cameo hand-made by a cousin of Ellie's who was the son of one of Son's older brothers. It was exquisitely made with a carved head set in gold. Very beautiful and by their standards very expensive we were told, about £25.

Then the carving of the warrior horseman was brought across the room and presented to us by its carver, a young cousin of the twins and a teacher at a local college. John and I were overwhelmed by this gift, especially as it had been made by a member of the family which obviously made it even more special. However, the same thought went immediately through both our minds – how the heck are we going to transport this around Australia for the next four weeks??? However, we will cross that bridge when we get to it. The statue almost instantly became known as Ghengis which seemed to be most appropriate despite the confusion of nationalities!

Again more speeches on both sides and I felt that I was beginning to get the hang of it! Making conversation was not easy and at one point we asked to see Huyen's school books to see what she was doing. John was surprised to see the level she had reached in mathematics where she could cope with simple algebraic equations that would have been alien to children in England at a similar age. We gave Ellie a quick public test on her tables (which she knew all the way through to 12 x 12) to show what a good grasp she had and Huyen, anxious to compete, snatched a pen to show that she could do just as well, if not better!

The rain continued but we eventually indicated that we would like to see outside. We were told that the present house was rebuilt in 1998 but set back several yards from its original position and, maybe, enlarged. This was made possible by using some of the money that we had been able to transfer to the bank account Margaret Daly had set up. There had also been sufficient to buy a cow (very similar to a Jersey), a couple of pigs and, eventually, a three-acre field. The toilet was to the right of the pig-sty and we all managed to avoid the necessity of using it for the entire day (thanks to the humidity), our imaginations working overtime – which proved to be accurate the following day! Across the courtyard was a small outhouse used for cooking where dried rice stalks were used to build a low fire on the floor, cooking apparently done in what looked like a couple of extremely large woks. Behind this outhouse was a seven-foot high 'haystack' made up of stalks from the harvested rice crop and clearly destined for cooking purposes and to one side was a brick well where water was collected by the traditional bucket on a rope.

Immediately behind and out of sight was the 'bathroom' – three walls open to the front and to the elements with a broken-brick floor. The 'bather' would collect water from the well on the way to this washing area – although we were led to understand that, in winter, warm water would be heated on the fire for some personal use. It was a situation we found hard to comprehend and so alien to what we were used to. We moved on to the house of Son's oldest brother about fifty yards away but to traverse the muddy flooded lane was not an easy task. This second house was built in the same style but above the TV was also a DVD – a fact which greatly amused us since this was something we still did not own at home! More tea – how much I hated it but needs must!

Some while after lunch Ghi's mother, in her eighties, left in the rain to go home on the back of her son's motorbike. It was a slightly incongruous sight and we just could not imagine such a thing happening at home. Apparently, it was many miles by road to Ghi's village (which we would be visiting tomorrow to meet the other half of the twins' family) but the motorbike was able to take a much shorter and quicker route by using a ferry or two to get over the intervening rivers.

Eventually we indicated that we would have to leave soon if we wanted to be back in Hanoi for 5.30pm. But it was 4pm when we finally left, no sadness as we would be returning the following day. The return journey was much quieter with less traffic and we turned our thought to the trip to Ha Long Bay where we would discuss the possibility of Huyen coming to England for her secondary education. We decided that Anh would try to negotiate a price for a bigger party on the boat so that we could take Phuong and Nam too since Dong would be at school. There would be ten of us altogether, we three, Son, Ghi and their three children and Anh and her son, Tuan, who was home on holiday from his degree course at Imperial College, London.

We reached the hotel in good time and the Tour Operator arrived at 6pm. Anh struck a good deal and we arranged that Phuong and Nam would be collected from Pho Moi en route to Ha Long Bay on Saturday – Son, Ghi and Huyen would already be with us as we had arranged that they would return with us to the hotel on Friday so that we could buy Huyen a bicycle. John and I had eaten quite well during the day and decided that we did not want more food but I needed to get a quick meal for Ellie who had eaten hardly anything. I was glad that I had brought some prepared meals, just in case! We all needed an early night after an exceedingly tiring day.

Friday 23rd July

We were again picked up by taxi at 8am but this time took the blue boxes with us. The driver was now familiar with the route and we arrived with no problems in far less time. We parked in the same place where wellies had again been arranged for us, a great idea for everyone except the pair designated to me was a fraction of the size of my huge feet. Needs must and I coped! The lane was well and truly flooded today; John gave Ellie a piggy back ride – causing some amusement and a lot of staring from family members and we wondered if such a method of carrying children was an alien concept for them. There still seemed to be as many people present as yesterday so, after a brief chat, we handed out the family presents which pleased everyone. Grandma, Son's mother, who was very stooped, looked great in her colourful scarf and John performed an amusing charade to show what benefits she would get from taking the one-a-day, high strength, cod liver oil we had also brought for her. It was extremely funny as he stooped like her, mimed taking a capsule and slowly stood up to his full height and started to caper around the room. Everyone thought this was extremely amusing although Grandma did look a little concerned. Whether she thought that the capsules really would have such an effect or whether she thought him mad was debatable!

It was soon 10am and we had to say goodbye as we were to visit Huyen's school next where the head and some staff were waiting to take ownership of the blue boxes although the school was actually closed to children for the summer holiday. The school was about a kilometre or so away and looked quite large, built in an almost colonial style facing onto a square playground marked out as a badminton court, it seemed. We were amazed to be told that it was used by around seven hundred children but seeming nowhere near large enough in comparison to Ellie's school at home. The reasons for this were made clear later when we learned that half the school attended a morning session and the rest an afternoon one. We were shown into the Director's office, a large but very bare room with little evidence of any paperwork and certainly nothing like a computer. We learnt that the school did not possess such equipment. Some parts of the school were very old although another building had been started a few hundred yards away for the older pupils but work had ground to a halt when money had run out. There was little sign of comfort in the staff room; at one end a bust of Ho Chi Min was set on a table – possibly as a shrine – and no easy chairs, just rows of long tables set up to resemble a lecture room but covered in the inevitable plastic cloths and an instant reminder of the leaving ceremony all those years ago.

We were told that the next room we visited was a library-cum-equipment room. There were a few bookcases containing dusty books and in another cabinet some bats and balls. An air of gloom pervaded over everything and I had yet to see a primary colour except on the gaudy table-cloths! Back outside we were shown the toilet block – a small sandy area was enclosed by some low brick walls which the children stood behind with virtually no privacy. No sit-down toilets, not even a hole on the ground a la French camping site. The staff were lucky, their toilet walls were marginally higher! We crossed the brick courtyard, the only place where any sport could take place, and reached a long, low building that looked reminiscent of a cow shed. One of the very old doors was padlocked so we peered through a small, barred window, unable to make out very much of the gloomy interior. With this the caretaker appeared, a key produced and we entered Huyen's classroom.

Words could hardly describe it. The electricity, we were told, was switched off for the holiday period and so the only light was limited to that coming in through a few narrow and glassless slits in the two side walls. At the front was a dais with a heavily pitted and not-very-black blackboard attached to the end wall and to one side the teacher's desk – the tall version so familiar to anyone who was at school in the 1940s and '50s – but soaking wet from the rain dripping in through the roof. Beyond were two rows of long wooden desks with bench seats attached, the sort that junior school children in the UK would have recognised as the norm fifty or more years ago. The dirt floor was extremely uneven with an enormous 'pothole' about a metre square towards the centre. Everything looked as though it was fit only to be scrapped and the brightest colour had to be the faded chalk on the blackboard.

The scene could not have been more depressing and any comparison with Ellie's school was impossible to make. John quietly remarked to me that he would think twice about keeping a horse in such a place. We were told that thirty-eight children used this classroom in the morning and a similar number in the afternoon. How the teachers could produce children with an education to Huyen's standard with so little stimulation and resources seemed an utter mystery to us.

But, clearly, the children responded well to their teachers and the homework desk back at the house seemed to suggest that parents saw education as being important. It seemed obvious to us both that children's behaviour and work-ethic coupled with parental support is far more important than computers, dumbed-down examinations and self-expressive behaviour in British schools. We seem to have lost the plot over recent years. Can the genie ever be put back in the bottle?

It was soon time to return to the car and we negotiated a rather long and tortuous journey to Ghi's childhood village to meet all her family, a journey of around thirty miles since the ferries were obviously unable to cope with anything larger than a motorcycle and we had to take the long way round. The flooded pathway leading to the house was about a hundred yards long and went round two sides of a sunken and water-filled area that looked as if it contained watercress. Planks had been placed on bricks to form a walkway over the path and we suspected that this was just for our benefit.

There were about thirty of Ghi's relatives present from the oldest man (her great uncle, we were led to believe) at ninety-three to a small baby. The house was much smaller than Son and Ghi's and seemed to be much poorer. Certainly, there was less surrounding land and the main room was probably about half the size. Because the day was so advanced (1pm) they had already eaten but more food was brought in for us to eat at a low table similar to that we had encountered at the first house. It was a veritable feast yet again (accompanied, unfortunately, by the ubiquitous small flies) and this time Ellie ate a little more. The inevitable speeches began with Ghi's brother-in-law, as the head of the family, thanking us for our return visit and, again, I took the lead replying in the same effusive manner whilst pausing for Anh's translation breaks which gave me time to think what I was going to say next! The girls were each presented with a silver bracelet from their maternal grandmother, Ellie still as shy as she had been the day before.

Finally, to our absolute consternation, we were presented with an enormous wooden eagle, some four feet high with spread wings arching over its recent kill and which had been lurking at the back of the room although neither of us had managed to spot it. This made Ghengis look positively miniature but we quickly succeeded in disguising our immediate concerns as to how this carving was also to be borne around large parts of Australia during the ensuing four weeks! This gift had been purchased rather than made by a family member and we were slightly relieved when it was pointed out that both arched wings were detachable. This would slightly reduce our transport problem. Taking it back to England would have proved difficult enough but lugging these two carving around Australia might be a bridge too far. Anyway, it would have been churlish to refuse. We felt that where there was a will there was always a way and it was something that we could sort out later.

We then had to visit the house of a nearby relative, something they were always keen for us to do, but we declined the offered tea since time was moving quickly on. It was 3pm when we left and, unfortunately, Ghi was very car-sick and, after a couple of stops, she moved to the front passenger seat. We arrived back at the hotel at 4.30pm and showed Son, Ghi and Huyen to their room – first making sure that they understood how the toilet worked (since it was the first time they had seen a flush system) and also how the bath filled.

There was just enough time to go out to look for a bicycle for Huyen, something we had promised to buy her, whilst we still had the benefit of Anh's help. We discovered a large shop selling all sorts of items quite close to the hotel with a vast selection of bikes. Far from being displayed in the European manner they all seemed to be leaning against one another and, of course, the one Huyen was particularly interested in was right at the back so some dozen or more bikes had to be moved to get to it! It was a silver, adult-sized bike, far too big really but one that would last her for many years. Apparently, there are no such things as children's bikes in the country. We paid about £10 and, as quick as a flash, Huyen was outside and pedalling off down the pavement in the standing position since the machine was too big for her to reach the pedals when sitting on the saddle.

John immediately ran after her since he was very concerned that her road sense was probably very limited, certainly in Hanoi traffic when she was only used to the quiet trackways of Vu Duong. The bike was duly left in the hotel foyer after the inevitable photographs and Anh left to go home at 5.45pm. After a quick shower and a rest, we left again to search for food and deciding that the pizza restaurant was as good a bet as any. Unfortunately, the rain was heavy and somehow we got lost so taking ages to get there.

It was not easy to communicate at all with Son or Ghi without Anh there to translate because none of us could speak a word of the others' language and we were a rather sombre group when we finally arrived. Not a good choice of venue. Son valiantly ate his bolognaise but Huyen was not a lover of something so strange as pizza and Ghi ate very little of her food indeed, would hardly try any of it. She rather strangely had hardly a word for Son or Huyen but engaged one of the waiters in a very animated conversation. Very odd! However, the real success was the ice-cream bar which both twins relished.

Conversation had been stilted throughout the meal and we were all glad to return to the hotel at 9pm. The family went off to their room and John and I packed ready for the Ha Long Bay break the next day.

26

Ha Long Bay

Saturday 24th July
Since we had a one hundred mile drive to Ha Long Bay we were leaving at 8am and had to be up early and breakfasted on bread and boiled eggs whilst the family had noodle soup. Wonderfully, it was not raining and we left on time in a 10-12 seater minibus with Huyen's bicycle squeezed in behind the back seat. It was a comfortable vehicle with all the appearance of being very new. Mindful of her previous bout of car-sickness, we put Ghi in the front passenger seat but neither this ploy nor the tablets I gave her before we left had any effect and the driver had to stop on two occasions along the way. We picked up Nam and Phuong who were waiting, as arranged, at the crossroads in Pho Moi along with Dong who was there to take the bicycle back to Vu Duong.

The road we travelled on was wide with peasant farmers already working the paddy fields on either side with the ubiquitous graves much in evidence. We passed small clusters of houses and shops from time to time and, at one point, the driver had to negotiate around half a dozen cows and calves lying on the tarmac in the middle of the road. John was particularly interested to note at least two seemingly working lime kilns and determined to stop on the way back to investigate one of them further.

We eventually drew onto the harbour side at Hai Phong at 11.30am and immediately saw how busy it seemed and how 'touristy', too. A large number of junks were moored side by side with bows to the quay with others moored in other ranks beyond them. All were painted the same mahogany colour and each had a different figurehead, mainly birds and animals. At this point the rain began again so we scrambled out of the bus and entered a low, single-storey glass waiting room whilst Anh went to sort out the boat. One was available immediately but she noticed that it seemed to be leaking rainwater and decided that we should wait for a better one which would, apparently, be available in about half an hour. It was very hot inside the waiting room but a little cooler than the humid atmosphere outside. The four children enjoyed an ice-cream and wandered round and we could see other people looking at the twins as they realised that one appeared to speak only Vietnamese and the other only English. Finally, we were able to climb onto a very smart-looking Chinese junk by carefully negotiating the decks of various other vessels.

Apparently, our boat had only been on three previous voyages and was virtually brand new. There were seven high-quality *en suite* cabins each equipped for four people so we had loads of space. Four of the cabins were sited on the lower deck and accessed by a gangway running around the outside of the vessel. The others were at the rear of the dining area on the middle deck and were occupied by the family. At the other end of the dining room there was a large and airy 'lounge' with a bar and this opened onto a small deck at the bow end and from where we could reach the upper deck via a steep companionway. We left immediately, powered by the junk's engine but very soon stopped out in the bay, short of the mountain tops and still in sight of the shoreline, in order to have lunch. The crew laid up the large and beautiful wooden tables in the dining room with white linen tablecloths and napkins. We were then served a meal which was truly incredible; dish after dish of crab, king prawns, beef and ginger, rice, soup, numerous fruits and even wine. We were well and truly sated!

We moved on and, by 2.30pm, the rain had finally stopped and we were able to go up on deck where there were several very comfortable teak lounging chairs and it was most pleasant to watch the world go slowly by. Gradually the weather began to warm up and we even saw a hazy sun for the first time since we had arrived from England. We passed several other boats and, as the coastline disappeared into the distance, we gradually entered the realm of an 'island' kingdom (in reality, mountain tops) that was almost impossible to describe; vast pieces of towering rock, some rising to 100m to 200m in height, which were totally uninhabited and, seemingly, scaleable only by a very experienced climber and topped with greenery rather like the icing on a cake. They had been formed, apparently, from decayed lateritic mountains – formed by the weathering of rocks in tropical regions. Around a thousand have names and at least two have breathtaking cave systems to rival anything in the IK. Strangely, there seemed to be an almost complete absence of birds of any kind.

Our first stop was at Su Sot Island where we landed to see the first famous cave system. Ghi had eaten very little for lunch and was now asleep so only nine of us ventured ashore.

The caves were truly magnificent. Three vaulted caverns filled with impressive stalactites and stalagmites and many other interesting formations, many of which were carefully illuminated from various angles by a series of coloured lights to accentuate the natural colours of the rocks or the shapes of the features. The atmosphere inside was still humid and certainly not cold, as we had anticipated. Back on the boat we were content to lounge and watch the unfolding scenery, aware that what we were seeing was unique in all the world and presented an opportunity we might never experience again. It seemed strange to us that Son, Ghi and the children took little or no interest in their surroundings – perhaps surprising since they had, we assumed, never had a holiday of any kind before. John and I, on the other hand, were absolutely mesmerised by the scenery and those surroundings and I was so pleased that he had followed his desire to come here.

Son and Ghi continued to have no conversation with one another whatsoever and were sitting some way apart. He eventually fell asleep and Anh was then able to conduct a quiet conversation with Ghi about her situation within the family and the marriage. Anh relayed the gist of Ghi's remarks to me and was able to confirm that she was very unhappy in the marriage and the contents of her letter to us back in April still applied. She confirmed that she had been persuaded by her mother and brother-in-law to withdraw her original allegations in her subsequent letter. Ghi was very clear that she would like Huyen to go to England for her schooling although John and I could not possibly have considered parting with Ellie if the boot had been on the other foot.

The weather was now extremely pleasant and, to us, verging on the 'quite hot'. We were absolutely delighted when, at 5pm, one of the crew arrived on deck with a tray containing oranges and two other exotic-looking fruits that we had never seen before. One, called dragon fruit, was particularly strange being cut into wedges like a melon but with a red skin and with tiny, black seeds dotted amongst the pure white flesh.

The captain was still using the engine and it was a source of regret to us that the wind was never strong enough for him to deploy the junk's sail. That would have been a wonderful memory to take home with us but it did not happen throughout the trip. However, at this point, John indicated to the captain that he would like to steer the junk and did so for around half an hour much to the amusement of the good-natured crew.

Ellie and I got out our pack of Uno cards and taught and played with the other children and Tuan and Phuong. This was a good ice-breaker that knew no language barriers and great fun was had by all – especially Ellie who seemed to be on a never-ending winning streak.

At 6.30pm we moored for the night in a small bay – actually a stretch of water encircled by mountain tops (just how deep is the water in the bay?) and completely out of sight of all other vessels. Some of the crew began to prepare the evening meal. We were now able to take the opportunity to swim so Son, Tuan, Nam, Ghi and both girls donned life jackets whilst John and I preferred to be without. Entry was via a ladder hooked onto the side of the boat although John and I decided to dive in. It was the first time Huyen had ever been in water and she loved it. It was only Ghi's second time since she told us she had swum in the river ten years ago whilst tending her parents' cow and buffalo when she had lived at home. She had tied them to a bamboo first so they could not stray! The water was a dark green in colour, not particularly cold, but very refreshing.

The boys struck out for the shore about a hundred yards away and clambered on the rocks at the water's edge whilst the rest of us were more circumspect, especially as

Huyen and Ghi were initially rather nervous of venturing too far away from the side of the junk. Phuong watched from the side of the boat and could not be persuaded to join us.

We stayed in the water for about twenty minutes and then had to hurry to be ready for our meal at 7.30pm. This was another sumptuous feast of chicken soup, fish/rice cakes, king prawns and a chicken dish with rice. It was all so incredibly tasty and impossible to believe that it had been prepared in a tiny galley at the back of the boat. At 8.30pm John, Ellie and I were ready for bed as we were so tired. The day had gone really well apart from Ghi's travel sickness and the fact that the food was apparently far too rich for her. She had eaten very little apart from rice at either meal.

Sunday 25th July

After a good night's sleep (during which we dreamily heard rain pattering on the deck above our heads) we had a substantial breakfast at 8am consisting of bread, cheese, omelettes and fruit. Tuan slept in until 10am and the rain finally stopped around midday. We spent time after breakfast sitting in the dining area and talking to Son and Ghi about Sidcot School and showing them the new parents' brochure whilst explaining all that the school had to offer. It was a long and frank discussion with Anh interpreting well, the outcome being that they were willing for Huyen to go to England in 2007 and would prepare her for the trip with English lessons beforehand.

This was certainly an amazing result and one we had not dared to hope would happen. We showed them photographs of our house and took them from room to room through the camcorder and especially pointing out the bedroom that Huyen would occupy. Afterwards, relieved that we had finally got the main purpose of our trip out of the way, we were able to settle into enjoying the break and relaxing completely. We played Donkey and Uno with the girls, Phuong, Nam and Tuan before we arrived at our first stop of the day, Tiptop Island, at 11.30am. Ghi stayed on board whilst John, Ellie, Huyen and I climbed the four hundred and twenty two steps to the Pagoda at the top where the view was staggering with islands and rocks stretched away into the distance in all directions in an almost surreal fashion shrouded in mist and thus appearing to rise mysteriously from the calm waters. We tried to take photographs of the girls together but Huyen was totally reluctant and, after hiding her face for several minutes, she suddenly zoomed off back down the steps with us in hot pursuit as we tried to catch her up, all the while calling to her to stop. We were not best pleased with her refusal to come back to us!

At the bottom John, Ellie and I swam in a cordoned-off area off a small sandy beach and Huyen quickly joined us wearing her life jacket. She had a wonderful time with no apparent fear of the water. Back on board the junk, we up-anchored and moved away to a quiet spot for lunch, another wonderful meal with many courses and, again, delicious King prawns. After lunch we went up to the top deck where we lounged and I chatted with Ghi and Son with Anh interpreting as usual and where I learned, for the first time, all about the twins' birth. Apparently, Son and Ghi were totally unprepared for twins and only found out when Huyen was delivered and the doctor said, in effect, 'Hang on. There's another'. Huyen had weighed just 1.8 kilograms whilst Ellie was only 1.2 kilograms. Neither side of the family had a history of twins, as far as anyone knew.

When Nam, the youngest, was about five years old, Son's first wife had left the family and he had subsequently

221

met Ghi some six months later when she had taken vegetables to sell at the local market. She felt sorry for him and they were soon married with Ghi falling pregnant a year later. She gave birth to a full-term baby girl who died a few hours later. In her second pregnancy, Ghi seemed to be very large and uncomfortable from the third month so she cut down on her food intake – a decision which could have been disastrous, as it turned out.

The twins had been kept in hospital for a week, not because of their low weight as would have been the case in England, but because Ghi was very unwell. Two months later they returned to the hospital for some medication for one of the older children and the doctors were amazed that both babies were still alive. Because the weather had turned cold, they kept both babies warm by placing plastic bottles filled with warm water next to them. This continued right up until the day when Ellie came to live with us at the Dream Hotel.

Ellie, apparently, was the baby chosen to be adopted because she cried a lot whilst Huyen was very much quieter. This, Son and Ghi concluded, meant that she had a good pair of lungs and would be healthy. Huyen, they told us, would cry easily as she grew up and would become moody and, on these occasions, would go off on her own and talk to no-one. She had many friends and was a very independent child, having learnt to bathe, wash her hair and dress herself since she was about five years old. Once she had been taken to Ghi's mother's for a few days but had missed her friends and had wanted to go home. It was fascinating seeing the similarities and differences between the two girls, filling in the details we had not previously known.

After lunch, the captain restarted the engine and we got under way again. The scenery was constantly shifting as we rounded every 'island' but we were totally unprepared for the sight of a floating village out, apparently, in the middle of no-where. Around twenty or more single storey huts, seemingly supported by plastic drums that probably had had a previous use, clustered in an area covering several acres. Anh, who told us that she had visited the area before, pointed out the village school which was painted yellow – the children presumably arriving by the many (presumably family owned) 'skiffs' we could see moored alongside the various huts and which we had previously seen with one or two people – frequently couples – fishing, perhaps for their own consumptions or maybe for trade.

The junk headed for one of the larger huts and as we got nearer we could see that there were several tanks tied alongside and largely below water level. Eventually, we could see that they contained fish. A man and, presumably, his teenage son, were working at the side of one of the tanks and, as we disembarked, we could see that they were tying up the claws of a large number of small crabs. Anh told us that fish is often exported, live, to other countries such as Japan. As far as we could understand, the fish could survive for long periods in cold water in tanks where the surrounding air pressure had been reduced. Apparently, the Bay is rich in fish and sea foods. One of the junk's crew proceeded to purchase a selection whilst John and I explored this tiny island trading post. We were very taken with a very attractive young woman sitting in an area apparently set aside for food and drinks for passing tourists. Presumably the man's wife, her fingernails were incredibly long and painted in a vast array of different colours that looked completely out of place in this somewhat austere and isolated place. We could only wonder if they were real or false!

At 3.30pm we arrived at Hang Dau Go island and

visited the caverns which were certainly the best we had seen so far. This time, we all left the boat so it was the first time Ghi had seen such a sight. She found it really exciting and clung to my arm all the way through the system. Coloured lights highlighted the rocks and official guides were on hand to point out the names of the different formations on view. Outside there were ice-creams for the girls and we set off again to find a quiet bay for the night. Afternoon tea, again at 5pm, with tea and different fruits from yesterday. At 6pm we stopped and swam again although Son declined along with Phuong – yet again – and John stayed on board to record the scene for posterity although the battery on his camcorder ran out after only a few minutes! It was great fun with Ghi and Huyen growing in confidence all the time. The evening meal was another huge meal with fried squid, spring rolls, stir-fried cabbage, chicken and rice amongst the dishes and followed by fresh pineapple. We again played cards until 9.30pm and chatted with Son who was a little concerned that Huyen would be behind at school due to her lack of English. We assured him that we thought she would quickly catch up with extra help. It was very hot during the night and John began having stomach cramps and the start of what was obviously an upset stomach.

Monday 26th July

Breakfast was again at 8am but we would be having an early lunch at 10.15am since we would be leaving the boat at noon. John stayed in bed with an extremely upset stomach. We could only think that he had eaten something that had disagreed with him. Luckily, both Ellie and I seemed to be okay.

We had to vacate our cabins by 10am so it was a rush to get John up and packed in time. When lunch arrived I was still feeling rather full. It was, again, the usual feast and as we ate we could view Bai Chai harbour and Han Gai city bathed clearly in sunshine. After the meal Ghi gave a long thank you and said how happy we had made her with this trip – somewhat of a surprise to us since she had apparently shown little interest in her surroundings from start to finish. However, she and I had formed quite a close relationship despite the language barrier and at this point we both had a little cry. John and I felt it was important to discuss the money that we had been sending out since Ghi had indicated that it was being used by Son for the older children and not for Ghi and Huyen, as intended. Anh translated that we wished Ghi to have twenty percent of the money in future to do as she wished with. Son agreed so we can only hope this works. Ghi had also made us aware, via Anh, that the children did little to help her in the house so we asked that this also be addressed. There is really very little that we can do to monitor or control this division of the money but we hoped it might make Ghi's life happier and somewhat easier.

We had moored just outside the rock formations and in sight of the coastal towns whilst we ate our final meal on the boat but then got under way again on our final approach to the harbour where we finally took up a berth amongst the many other junks already moored up. The trip had certainly been a huge success as far as we were concerned. It had given us a breathing space where we were able to relax and the opportunity to speak to Son and Ghi in a neutral environment which we could not have created elsewhere.

We said goodbye to the four-man crew who had been excellent but then, unfortunately, we had to wait around an hour and a half in the waiting room without air-conditioning. The twins play-fought and grunted at one another

– their method of communication – and ate ice cream. The heat was stifling. We tourists watched, noting the many back packers – mainly young couples – but even seeing a few families with very young children. One European couple even had a very young fair-headed baby who was being breast fed. I certainly would not have wanted to bring such a young infant here but maybe they were working locally. We thought how different it was for them now as opposed to when we were first in Vietnam eight years ago. Then, in 1996, we truly felt as though we had been intrepid explorers and trail-blazers. Finally the minibus arrived and we had an uneventful trip back without Ghi suffering car sickness. At one point John asked the driver to stop so he could film at one of the lime kilns that he had noticed at the side of the road a couple of days before on our way to Ha Long Bay.

The kiln was situated on the side of a small creek and a pile of coal had been dumped, presumably from a barge, half in and half out of the water. One man was shovelling the coal into two raffia baskets which were then carried by two other men on their backs across to the bottom of the kiln and then up a narrow stone staircase on the side before being tipped into the open top of the kiln. Both men were black down their backs and legs where the water continually drained out of the coal and mixed with their sweat. A fourth man was breaking lumps of limestone into smaller pieces with a sledgehammer. It was a scene probably last seen in England about a hundred years ago. The four men were working steadily in the blistering heat. Beside this kiln was a second one which they would, presumably, switch to when the first was full. John had had the camcorder battery on charge over night so, mindful of the niceties, was able to indicate the camera and seek their permission to film them. The men were all clearly thrilled and, grinning hugely, all four posed for him. He then had to indicate that he wanted to record them at work and they cheerfully went back to what they were doing for a few minutes. No doubt they were pleased to have the monotony of their work broken for a short while. John then sought their permission to climb to the top of the kiln to examine and film the interior – afterwards describing the intense heat it was giving off. Before he returned to the minibus the men indicated that they would like to see themselves on film and John was pleased to show them what he had recorded. Members of the family got out of the minibus to watch – no doubt wondering what all the fuss was about!

Ghi had decided that she would go home rather than return to Hanoi for the night, as planned. Feeding the cow was used as an excuse but, maybe, she just felt uncomfortable away from the environment that she knew most intimately. We stopped at Pho Moi so she could get out and return to Vu Duong on the pillion of a motorcycle-taxi and the rest of us continued on to the hotel, arriving at 3.30pm. John bailed out in the city centre to change some money and collect a new pair of glasses he had ordered from a prescription brought from Weston-super-Mare for the purpose. In fact, these glasses were especially needed since he had somehow lost his previous pair on the journey from Heathrow and could only conclude that he had somehow left them behind at Changai airport when we changed planes at Singapore. Tuan went with him to translate during this transaction and then went on to his own home. Phuong was captivated by the scenery in Hanoi; neither she nor Nam had ever been beyond Pho Moi before and the traffic even there had been sufficient to scare her!

27

Last Goodbyes

At the hotel Anh offered to return at 7am next day in order to take the family to see Ho Chi Minh's mausoleum. We decided that we would probably join them. We all went to our rooms to shower since it was so hot and sticky and John returned shortly after. His glasses would be ready the next day for a mere £35, what service! The girls amused themselves by running between the bedrooms and playing cards. I offered to take the family out to eat but they declined and ate locally at a small café just along the road and probably eating food they were far more comfortable with! John was not up to having any food and Ellie and I were content to have a snack pot each for convenience.

I rang Mum in Exmouth who was really surprised to hear from me. She was due to have a cataract operation performed but it had been cancelled because she had developed a leg infection. It was good to speak to her and reminded me of phone calls all those years before when hearing a familiar voice was a real lifeline. A little later, at 8.45pm, Ellie and I went for a walk and the differences from previous occasions were very noticeable. The road outside was alive with people sitting at numerous low tables eating and drinking. The pedestrianisation has obviously made a huge difference and the local restaurant owners had been quick to cash in on trade. I walked a few yards up the street to look at the narrow block that was being built last time we were here. It was now offices with a smart bank exchange below. We completed our short circuit by returning along the railway line, a first for me and most interesting to see how people lived just ten feet from the actual rails. We were all ready for bed at 9.30pm after a very long and tiring day.

Tuesday 27th July

Ellie and I were up early for the visit to the Mausoleum. It certainly made more sense to go early when it was cooler and there were likely to be less people. Anh had ordered a taxi for us but John's stomach was still badly upset and he decided that it would be prudent to stay close to the hotel. However, even at that comparatively early hour there were many people queuing and, eventually, marshalled by officials into two long lines. Vietnamese citizens were allowed in free but I had to pay a nominal fee.

Unfortunately, I had given little thought to my clothes and had dressed for the weather in shorts and an armless top so I had to buy a cheap t-shirt and then don a sari-type length of gaudy cotton cloth handed to me by an official which I was able to wrap around my waist. It was already very hot and the queue moved very slowly. Bags had to go through a security screen and, together with cameras and mobile phones, left behind so that no-one was carrying anything. I had grave doubts about being reunited with everything but had little choice. As always, the staff were overly officious and we had to follow two painted white lines which eventually passed under the luxury of an awning.

At last, we arrived on the parade ground where soldiers in white uniforms were lined up. Just outside the entrance to the tomb they were carrying guns hoisted to the shoulder which added a sinister twist to the occasion. We filed slowly up the steps and shuffled inside, struck immediately by the icy coldness of the still air. The silence was almost total with not a word being spoken, broken only by the soft shuffling of feet as people inched forward. The coffin, about ten feet to our right, was raised up and open for all to see into. It was gloomy but still easy to see Ho as he lay with hands across his chest. Our route traversed three sides and all eyes were drawn to the diminutive and lifeless figure whose skin looked like alabaster. I experienced a sense of awe to be in the presence of such a national hero. If I could feel this then surely these feelings must have been intensified many times for those who share his nationality. All hats had been removed at the door and we were made to keep moving by the guards. No time to stop and stare!

Back outside we were hit by a wall of hot air in obvious contrast to the coldness we had just experienced. Our belongings were safely returned and we strolled along the path to see Ho's house beside the lake, a small, two-storey building almost colonial in appearance that we were only allowed to glance into. We stopped beside the lake so that Anh could take some group photographs for the family and then continued to the vast museum a little further on. All the displays had English sub titles and were most interesting – a bonus I had not expected. We queued for ice creams and then returned to the hotel by taxi as John was just getting up.

After he had breakfasted we all walked to the lake, collecting his new glasses on the way. Another ice cream of coconut milk, at 3,000 dong or about 12p a real bargain! We continued on to the new department store on the corner of Tran Tien where we found the air conditioning truly amazing in the day's heat. Phuong was in awe of the whole place and very nervous about ascending in the scenic lift. We then tried out the escalators and a cautious Phuong needed my arm to help her get on and off, finding it very difficult to master the timing and balance required. We were able, whilst we were there, to have some links removed from the watch strap we had given Son but which was clearly too big for him.

We strolled back around the lake and then waited to collect a bus back to the hotel, something we would not have done without Anh's help.

On our return, John excused himself, his stomach still not well, whilst the rest of us chatted and said goodbye. Anh took the family out for some food and then was to drop them at a bus stop so they could catch the bus back to Pho Moi, a journey of about an hour. We will see them again on Friday for the last time so spent the rest of the day relaxing in our room, playing cards and catching up on diaries. Ellie also enjoyed listening to some of her story tapes. John was still not up to eating so Ellie and I had a quick snack and then went out for some fresh air. We were both horrified to spot an enormous rat scoot off the top of an upright freezer just inside a small restaurant on the other side of the road, neither of us daring to believe what we had seen until the other confirmed that our eyes had not deceived us! This little restaurant looked quite smart so appearances were definitely deceptive! The smells in the street are as varied as always but are beginning to turn my stomach now, I'm certainly not hungry. We turned into Hang Bong and took the second left to bringing us up to the shops below the indoor market where we had previously bought the baked beans, such vivid memories. The air tonight was close and warm, stepping out of the coolness of our room had been

231

like entering a sauna. Thank goodness for the delights of air conditioning! We completed our circuit ready for baths, a drink and an early night.

Wednesday 28th July

John was not at all well again today so Ellie and I were on the baked bean hunt! After breakfast we walked to Hang Da market to look at the stalls where I had found them in 1995. No luck this time! We saw many animals in cages; dogs, cats and even a monkey which really upset Ellie. One small bucket half filled with water held three small turtles and their fate could only be guessed at. We took a cyclo to the department store – Ellie's first ride so very exciting for her. I bartered and paid 15,000 dong for the journey, not really happy doing it but felt that the larger sum being asked for was an exploitation of tourists. The store did not look promising either. We picked up yoghurts, biscuits and even Pringles and then on one last look in the European section Ellie spied some red tins of American beans for only 14,500 dong, about 58p, so we bought two and also some hand cream for Ghi who we felt desperately needed it. We walked round the lake but finding the heat so intense I hired another cyclo to return to the hotel, this time for 20,000 dong.

At 2pm, Ellie and I went out again. My intention this time was to visit an old house situated in the Old Quarter which had only recently been opened to the public. Such things had not existed in 1995 and it was interesting to see how the country is beginning to adapt to the expectations of tourists. In sweltering heat we walked up Hang Gai where I would have loved to have browsed in the shops but, yet again, was thwarted by the pushiness of the shop keepers so I gave up. It is sad that some of them feel the need to press items on potential customers as I am sure that they would sell far more stock if they let people browse. We eventually found the house but as we were both so hot and thirsty we first went into an internet café opposite for some delicious juices and a chocolate ice cream for Ellie. It seemed strange to see so many European ideas in place and facilities such as internet cafes were a draw for Europeans of all nationalities as well as for many young Vietnamese.

The house was quiet, cool and interesting. We had to remove our shoes to go upstairs and were given a short guide written in English. It was certainly not a residence for the poorer inhabitants of Hanoi! In one small room was a collection of inexpensive souvenirs so I purchased a black beaded bag for my niece. By now, Ellie had had enough of culture so we returned to the hotel by cyclo again. We had been invited to dine with Anh and her husband in the evening and were to be collected by Tuan at 6pm so we all had time to relax first. A bath or shower was always required after any journey outside the hotel! John looked awful but was determined to go.

When Tuan arrived, we elected to go by taxi since no-one could entertain the thought of a walk in that heat. We were set down on the other side of a wide road opposite the old quarter, near a new foreign bank. We stopped in a side street and then walked into a small alley where there was a large communal area under a block of ten-year old flats. The stairway was unlit and we went up four flights until we came to their flat on the left. It was small, just three rooms and a bathroom and no air conditioning either. Anh's husband, Dom, was a good looking man and seemed to have that youthful appearance that we had seen in so many of the men. The lounge-cum-dining room was smallish by European comparison and had a fridge in one corner. Anh's nephew, a young man about twenty years old, was also present, living with them whilst he attends college in Hanoi. He did know some English but was reluctant to use it. We sat and chatted to Tuan with some orange juice until the food, prepared in a tiny kitchen off, was ready. There was soup, a kind of spring roll, beef, fish squares and a very tasty salad. John managed to eat a little of each and Ellie had some rice but little else! Afterwards there was dragon fruit and plums, the whole meal washed down with a very nice burgundy. Shortly after, Dom disappeared only to return about five minutes later with some pills that he had bought for John to settle his stomach. Only about 1000 dong (4p) for 100! There was also some cream for Ellie's ankle which was very red and swollen from a mosquito bite. Anh presented both Ellie and me with a small silver box each and we passed over the silver necklace we had bought her from England. Such a very small thing for someone who had done so much for us! We left at 8.30pm by taxi, all ready for another early night.

Thursday 29th July

John appeared to be much better this morning having taken the magic pills prescribed by Dom. Since they were so tiny it was amazing to see how effective they were! John had his beloved beans for breakfast and then we went on a hunt for large boxes to pack the carvings in for the next leg of our journey to Sidney and, subsequently, to three other centres of our four-week Australian holiday. He had originally planned to dismantle the eagle by removing the detachable wings but was now concerned about the distribution of weight. So it was back to plan A, a box for each of them to spread that weight. We were only successful in finding one for the smaller statue (always now referred to as Genghis) but having chatted to some young Australians we rethought the situation.

We searched in the largest bookshop for a map showing Vu Duong but could only find the village in a book . Instead we bought some English books to help Huyen to study in preparation for her trip to England in 2007 and also managed to buy some string and tape for the boxes which in itself was a huge achievement. We returned to the hotel as it was now becoming quite hot and John was still not feeling 100%. Later I went to visit The Temple Of Literature on my own, determined that I would visit some of the sights this time round. Inside it was cool, calm and fascinating, the age of the building reminded me of all the history that belonged to this part of the world which was woven into Ellie's heritage.

Afterwards, I continued my walk and was surprised to see a funeral procession. The ornate coffin was placed in a mini bus whilst the people who had been walking behind then clambered in, too. Some had white cheese cloth over their faces and also their bodies. A young boy and girl, who had been walking backwards in front of the coffin holding up a large photo of presumably the deceased, then joined them. It was a most unusual spectacle and obviously full of ceremony that I did not understand. I returned to the hotel tired after all my walking.

At 6pm Anh had arranged to take Ellie and me to see a Chinese astrologer to have a horoscope prepared for her. This was something Anh was very keen to do and we felt it would be churlish to refuse what was obviously an honour she was bestowing on us since it would be prepared by a personal friend of hers. As it was some distance, we went by taxi and then spent some one and a half hours with the astrologer. I tried to write down all he had said so I could write it up at a later date. It was very hot in his small room and Ellie had some problem keeping still so I was thankful when we eventually left after giving a small donation of ten US dollars. We returned to the hotel at 8.30pm after a bus and cyclo ride by now both quite hungry!

Friday 30th July
Our last full day and one that would be very emotional. Luckily we all had a good night's sleep and were ready at 8.30am when Tuan arrived. Anh was not able to come to the village with us today as she had to be at her place of work but Tuan had volunteered his services as translator and we were indebted to him. We had the same driver as last week, a friend of the receptionist at the hotel. We had only been able to use him for the first day as his was a small car and we had been transporting members of the family on other occasions. Today it would just be Tuan and the three of us. The weather was very pleasant and it was good to view the scenery in a more positive light with the sun shining. The fields looked very green and the workers appeared colourful by contrast. We saw several people scooping water over small dykes using a swinging paddle suspended from a wooden tripod. A simple but very effective way to irrigate the paddy fields.

In Pho Moi we stopped to buy a bell for Huyen's bike having had no success in Hanoi. We bought the most expensive in the shop, only 5,000 dong, about 20p! Huyen was eagerly waiting to see us and had been up to the crossroads many times on her bike since 7am! She was wearing different clothes to the ones Son had asked for as he had wanted the girls to dress the same today, but as soon as we arrived she went into the house and changed. Both wearing stripped lilac and white t-shirts and lilac skirts made telling them apart even harder! We sat down at the low table and were given the inevitable tiny cups of tea. John went outside to film some of the exterior and the garden area and I handed out the items we had brought with us. A small, hand-held fan for grandma with extra batteries, the water pistols and books for Huyen, a body spray for Phuong and the hand cream for Ghi. We sat and chatted whilst Tuan performed a grand job of translating.

Today we could see the interior of the house more easily as there were fewer people present. We noticed that all the clothes the family possessed seemed to be hanging from hooks above the relevant bed, so very little each! We were able to work out who slept where: Son, Ghi and Huyen in the large bed beside the small table we sat at, the two boys in the one at the opposite end of the room and Phuong and grandma in the one in the small curtained-off room. Here we could see the rice silo where the harvested rice is stored. Son opened a small sliding flap at the bottom and gave me a handful of rice to take away. To the left was a long wooden desk similar to those in the school and where, presumably, all the children sat to do their homework. Above was a bare light bulb and a small fan hung from the ceiling. I looked at Phuong's books which were all very neat and tidy. The English text book looked very difficult and old fashioned in style and I suspected that she under-stood only a little.

At 11am it was time to eat and another real feast had been prepared; noodles, pork, chicken, some delicious parcels of meat wrapped in vine leaves followed by lychees, water melon and a type of sweet bean curd. We coped well with the chop sticks and the different flavours but, as always, Ellie struggled, reluctant to try anything new. Afterwards she was presented with a gift from one of her second cousins who was the son of Son's second brother. His name is Ninh and he is a very young-looking thirty-two year old, married with two young children. It was a VCD player and he plugged it into the TV to show us how it worked. The young children in the room sat down eagerly to watch the programmes on offer. We were truly overwhelmed by such a generous present which, according to Tuan, would have been worth a considerable amount of money to them.

At first we thought it was a DVD player but then quickly realised it was not. Our use for it in the UK would certainly be limited since VCDs have not really taken off and are in limited supply. Another present and another problem for us in our luggage, a thought that made us feel quite guilty. At least this is not quite so cumbersome as the statues! Apparently, the cousin runs his own TV/video repair shop, hence the gift. Ellie was presented with two coins from grandma, Son's mother, as keepsakes and also a 5,000 dong note from a friend of the family called Mr Vinh. We were fulsome in our thanks and touched by the generosity of all concerned.

We had indicated that we would like to tour the village as the weather was so much better today so we set off with Tuan, Son, Ghi, Dong, Nam and a gaggle of children. Son explained that the village was split into five areas: North, West, Centre, Pagoda and the East section where they lived. We moved up to the dyke, a raised bank running along the side of the river which served as protection for the village in times of flooding. Dong had borrowed a motorbike from a friend and the twins, who were encouraged to hop on the back, disappeared into the distance.

I felt rather nervous about the whole situation, such things as safety helmets feature little in Vietnamese life and I would not have allowed such a thing in England. Ellie, I knew, would be very nervous about being on her own in such a situation where she could understand no-one.

We strolled for about an hour and visited four families

including Ninh where we saw his small TV repair shop situated in a room beside the road at the front of his house. When we returned, Dong was still not back with the girls and we were rather anxious since Ellie would not be able to express herself in her present company. Phuong was sent to search for them. We were asked to visit the houses of both Son's brothers who lived next door and across the courtyard. They were all similar in style with Buddha shrines set up in the living room. By now, Ellie had been gone for some two hours but suddenly Dong appeared and, after being no doubt told that we had been rather anxious, apologised separately to both of us. I explained that it was Ghi he should be apologising to since he had limited her last contact with Ellie by a considerable amount.

As the time rapidly approached for us to leave I could see Ghi becoming increasingly quiet and my heart went out to her. It was now 2.30pm and John did not want to tarry much longer as he felt he could not trust his stomach upset. Neither of us had felt the call of nature during our stay in the village – no doubt aided by the humidity – but the pile of ash in the outside 'privy' made the remembrance of a French campsite loo almost affectionate!

The goodbyes began in the house. Huyen wished us a shy 'health and happiness'. Ellie replied saying that she hoped Huyen would come to school in England and then she wished happiness to all the family. She was asked if she would like to live here (a definite 'No') and then Huyen was asked if she would like to live in England to which she gave a definite 'Yes'! John said that he and I would make the decision and maybe we could leave Ellie here and take Huyen in her place which gained a big laugh – except from Ellie!

John also thanked Tuan for his time and expertise in translating so efficiently for us all and asked him to thank his mother, on behalf of the family and us, for all her help, kindness and interest. This was loudly applauded by everyone after he translated. Grandma was very upset and would not let go my arm. I suspected that she realized it might be her last chance to see any of us. We promised to send copies of all the photographs and left her bent over on the steps as we made our way out to the car, again parked in the neighbour's courtyard fifty yards away. Dong and Phuong were in floods of tears as, of course, were Ghi and Son. It was only Nam who did not cry. I gave Phuong a huge hug, she is such a lovely girl, and explained that she must work on her English so she can come to visit us in England one day. Our bags were put into the back of the car together with a plastic carrier bag with the head of a live chicken poking out – a present for Anh – and a large bag of fruit for us. We had to gently decline the chicken as Tuan felt there was no way his mother could cope with plucking it. It was politely left behind to live another day.

Finally, Ellie and Huyen embraced and said their goodbyes. It was such a poignant moment and Huyen was full of tears. Up to this point, Ellie had seemed very calm about the whole situation but now they clung together and it was heart-wrenching to see. At last, we were in the car clasping hands through the window and then slowly bumping away down the lane. We turned to see them all gathered together waving us away and at this point Ellie began to howl. Our beloved daughter had always seemed so distant and reluctant to show her feelings and now they came flooding out in a huge emotional torrent. John and I had tears streaming down our faces and Ellie's response made them flow even faster. It was dreadful, especially as I could empathise so completely with those we had left behind.

Ellie, no doubt emotionally exhausted, slept for most

of the journey back to the hotel and it was not until we neared Hanoi that we began to cheer up, slightly.

We said goodbye to Tuan, not sure if we would see him again but hoping that he would visit us for Christmas from his studies in London. We had our last trip to Pepperoni's where Ellie, who had eaten so little all day, managed a few chips now. It had been an incredibly emotional day and all the more tiring for that. I think that, in my mind, I had already said goodbye to Vietnam and was now looking to the next stage of our journey which would, hopefully, be more of a holiday than the emotional roller coaster we had just experienced!

Saturday 31st July

We had two hours to finish our packing and at times despaired that it would all go in. The eagle, with wings detached, went into one of the large suitcases. Genghis went into a cardboard box with head and one raised hoof sticking out the end and body well padded around with various items of clothing.

Everything was so different to the last time we left. Anh and Tuan arrived unexpectedly to say goodbye which was so thoughtful of them and we promised to keep in touch and to see Tuan in Weston. The journey to the airport had certain similarities but so much had changed from before. I closed my eyes and tried to remember how ecstatic I had been in 1996, coupled with the terror that something could still go wrong.

At the airport the modern toilets with automatic flush were a lifetime away from our previous memories and the range of duty free shops another indication of how much had changed in eight short years. Finally, we were on the aeroplane which took off at 2.10pm local time. So another chapter in our lives closed and, as I sat in my seat watching the passing images below of a country I had little hope of ever understanding, my mind went over all that had happened in the past ten days, an experience that so very few people would ever have. I still did not know whether returning had been the right thing to do but I suspected that Ghi would have been willing to trade all the sorrow at our departure for the short time when she was able to see her daughters reunited with her. We had proved we were as good as our word. We had kept that promise made all those years ago.

We returned from Australia after a wonderful four-week, four-destination holiday with friends and distant family members feeling happy that all had gone so well during our short stay in Hanoi. Our expectations of what we might have achieved in Vietnam had been easily met and we felt secure in our belief that Huyen's future visit to England was much more of a certainty than it had been just six weeks previously. We were, however, quick to warn Ellie that Huyen could change her mind at any stage and she should be prepared for disappointment if she did. 2007 still seemed an awfully long time ahead and it was easier to put it out of our minds and carry on as normal. In truth, we were both happy to settle back into our busy lives whilst enjoying watching and helping Ellie to develop still further.

28

2004 – 2007

Although she was becoming an intelligent and interesting child, life appeared not to be so easy for Ellie as she struggled to make friends at school. Although she was developing an excellent sense of humour with other children, especially those she did not know well, she was quiet and shy. However, she did form one very strong friendship which was to last for two and a half years but she was left devastated when that friend moved to the north of England with her family in June 2006 and all contact with Ellie was severed. For Ellie, that seemed to be the ultimate betrayal and a valuable lesson was learned the hard way about the fickleness of so-called friends.

As far as I was concerned, my teaching post became increasingly hectic and demanding as I struggled to retrain myself in two new subject areas, Food (the old Domestic Science) and Child Development. The latter was something that I really enjoyed learning about and, of course, I was able to bring into play my own experience with infertility and adoption. The purchase of a six-berth motor home in 2003 meant that we were then able to holiday more frequently and enjoyed several long summers touring

France. In 2005 and 2006 we made the long journey to Provence in south-east France to stay with our friends, Jacqueline and Antoine Saavadra, our first meetings since Hanoi 1996.

Ellie had begun horse riding lessons just before we went out to Vietnam in 2004 and she continued with this for several years showing considerable enjoyment and expertise. John would take her to lessons in the nearby village of Hutton where she started on small Shetland ponies but eventually, at a later riding school, went on to ride horses as big as fifteen hands or more and, on several occasions, an elderly 'bolter' that all the other children refused to even sit on! John took her to all these lessons every Saturday morning and always stayed to watch. Her progress was something to talk about in the car going home.

Ellie always took her riding kit to France and was able to enjoy lessons wherever we went – particularly when visiting the Saavadra children, Jeremy and Alice, who were also keen although rather more experienced riders. Lessons there were so much more fun (or should that be scary?) and daring than at home as less emphasis was placed on 'health and safety' issues. Ellie experienced riding without stirrups, without reins whilst controlling her horse with her knees, sitting backwards on the saddle, hanging out the side of it and playing competitive games on horseback – a complete change from the mundane and boring lessons at Hutton.

Jeremy, just nineteen days younger than Ellie, had grown into a handsome and lively boy although very small compared with European children of the same age. He had been joined by Alice, two years younger, who the Saavadras had adopted during a second visit to Hanoi in 1997. It was a real delight to see how happy they all were and what privileged lives both children led and enjoyed. The

Saavadra's modern, two-storey house in the small village of Caderousse, just north of Orange, had its own outdoor swimming pool where all three children played together. Although neither Alice nor Jeremy spoke a word of English and Ellie not a word of French, all three of them played happily together and chattered away to each other in their own language. Responses did not seem to be necessary! Jacqueline was always very generous with Ellie and insisted on buying her various items of clothing every time we saw them.

We invited the family to spend Christmas 2006 with us in Weston-super-Mare as a thank-you for their hospitality and were able to introduce them to our English traditions. The motor home was also to prove a superb 'children carrier' for birthday parties and sometimes gave us the opportunity to take a friend away for weekends with Ellie.

Ellie also began playing the violin and had regular lessons with a local teacher in Weston. She started with a half-size instrument and became increasingly skilful despite her small hands. Unfortunately, her shyness meant that our efforts to persuade her to join the Weston Youth Orchestra fell on deaf ears but she has continued with lessons at Sidcot School and achieved Grade 2 success in 2009.

She soon developed into an avid reader and always seemed to have her nose in a book. Her reading age was well in advance of her chronological age and she was clearly one of the top two or three in her class all the way through six years at Hutton Junior School. In fact, by the age of eleven she was able to produce top grades in all subjects in the Year 6 SATs tests.

During this period, the prospect of Huyen's impending arrival was pushed very much to the back of our minds but as the time drew nearer we began to envisage all sorts of problems that we had not previously considered. Huyen's arrival was obviously going to have a huge effect on Ellie and we were both concerned with the best way to limit this. Huyen's position in the family was something that we had given little thought to since she would be living here as Ellie's sister but as our ward and not as our daughter. She could never be Ellie's equal in our hearts. She was, after all, someone else's child and we would have to be very careful not to create a situation where we began to replace Son and Ghi in Huyen's affections. But would we be able to cope with the subtleties of such an arrangement and could Ellie and Huyen also cope?

The fees at Sidcot, which had appeared relatively manageable three years earlier had shown a steady increase in line with the national trend which would not have overly affected us when paying for one child – but paying for two would be quite another matter. These thoughts were still only half-formed background concerns and their full impact was to occur much later when Huyen had actually arrived.

Just before Christmas 2006 we learned of the death of Ellie and Huyen's paternal grandmother in Vu Duong which was something of a blessing for us since Huyen would, presumably, become accustomed to her loss before she left for England. It would also mean that Grandma would not suffer the loss of her granddaughter, with whom she was obviously very close.

The last three years had been an especially happy time for us as a family, both John and I settled in our jobs and routines with Ellie at the centre of our universe, but the end of an era seemed to be fast approaching. The changes that had seemed so far away were almost upon us.

29

2007 – Will Huyen Come With Us?

John had steadily been making plans for this visit from as early as January always, I suspected, believing that it would never actually take place because Huyen would surely change her mind at the last minute. The likelihood of her leaving her parents, maternal grandmother, siblings, her wider family and her whole way of life for such a mind-boggling unknown world such as ours would surely be too much for her to even contemplate. I knew that Ellie would never be able to make such a transition and it would take a tremendous amount of courage for Huyen to do so.

Our plans encountered a hitch early on when we discovered the difficulties involved in obtaining a United Kingdom visa for Huyen. Yet again it was brought home to us how difficult it is to gain lawful entry to the UK and the hoops that had to be jumped through. Our original intention had been to travel to Vietnam during the Easter break when Ellie and I would have had almost three weeks school holiday. This would ensure that collecting Huyen would be a somewhat leisurely experience and, more importantly, she would have the best part of five months to get her English up-to-speed before the Autumn school term started at Sidcot. However, we then discovered that a visa for Huyen to enter the UK could only be issued a maximum of three months prior to her starting date at a registered institute, which, in our case, would be Sidcot School. We tried desperately to find a registered teacher or a course at the local college which would fulfil the criteria but to no avail. The main problem seemed to be that Weston-super-Mare was playing host to many migrant workers and their families from Eastern Europe and, as a consequence, all the English-as-a-second-language courses were heavily over-subscribed. Additionally, the courses were designed for adults, not eleven year-old girls.

Eventually, we were given the name of Sue Southwell who had experience of teaching English as a foreign language but was no longer registered as such. Sue lived in the village of Bleadon, about four miles away, and readily agreed to take on Huyen for three two-hour sessions a week once she arrived in the UK. But this arrangement would not qualify as 'an approved course' so we had to change our plans and elected to travel out during the half term week at the end of May when all three of us could go together. This would be the earliest date we could obtain a visa for Huyen, being exactly three months before the start of Sidcot's scholastic year in September. It would mean that we would be travelling to Vietnam and back in just over a week – not the best of solutions but just feasible with the extra day my headmaster allowed me to take.

With our plans in place, the local council elections now took centre stage. John had been a founder member of the Weston-super-Mare Town Council since 2000 and a landslide victory for the Conservatives suddenly saw him elected Town Mayor for the coming twelve months with me as Mayoress and installation just ten days prior to our departure for Vietnam. I had no idea how either of us would cope but after a worrying few days decided that it was best to bite the bullet since, no doubt, all would eventually fall into place. The pomp and ceremony of Mayor-making was to contrast vividly with our later experiences in Vietnam just a short while later.

We left on Saturday 26th May with, again, another two blue polystyrene boxes, quickly packed with various items that Ellie had grown out of. This time we flew via Bangkok with Thai Airways as the fares were cheaper – a big mistake, as it turned out, since the plane had none of the in-flight entertainment we had previously enjoyed on Singapore Airlines and which our local travel agent had assured John was also available on Thai flights – and booked in again at the Dream 2 Hotel. Monday, 28th May saw us waiting at the hotel to meet the family so that they could accompany us to the British Embassy to arrange Huyen's visa. Conversation was impossible as we had no common language and no Anh today but they were pleased to see us again; Huyen and Ellie being understandably very shy together.

At the Embassy all seemed to be going swimmingly until we encountered a problem with our proof of income. John had bought our P 60's with him assuming this to be a fair reflection of our income but, apparently, a current bank statement was required since we were going to be financially responsible for Huyen whilst she was in the UK. Luckily, our account in England had a reasonably healthy balance and Embassy staff allowed us to telephone John's sister (at 5am English time!) to ask her to go to our house, find our most recent bank statement and fax us a copy. We arranged to return at 4pm and left to visit the Thai Airways office to check our return tickets.

Huyen's one-way ticket had been reserved by Anh several months earlier, a much cheaper option than buying it in England. We were soon faced with our second problem of the day when it transpired that Huyen's reservation had needed to be renewed by 22nd May. It hadn't been and so it had been cancelled – all news to us! Yet another problem to surmount. No problem on the Bangkok-England connecting flight but the Hanoi-Bangkok flight was full! However, we were able to make a reservation for all of us on an earlier flight to Bangkok which meant a seven hour stop-over when we got there – not ideal but better than nothing.

Later, we returned to the Embassy after seeing the family off to Vu Duong at the bus stop. It was so very different from the colonial-styled Embassy building of our 1996 memories. The Embassy is now sited in the centre of the city and on the fifth floor of a modern office block with maximum security and the hi-tech efficiency associated with the 21st century. Gill had telephoned to check that her fax of our latest bank statement had arrived but, apparently, there was a glitch somewhere in the system and it had not been received by the Embassy staff. It was arranged that she would repeat the exercise and we said that we would return in a couple of days.

Tuesday 26th May: Today we visited the village – with Anh to translate – to meet all the family and spend some time with them. At 3pm Huyen's classmates arrived for a small party and to say goodbye to her. This time we knew what to expect and coped reasonably well with the heat and the food. The children sang a local song to us and requested a reply. We managed "Old Macdonald had a farm" – giving a sterling performance which included plenty of animal noises and actions! We finally left at 4pm taking Ghi and Son with us for a short way so we could visit Grandma's grave on the outskirts of the village. It was sited near the river, just a mound of earth which would be dug up after three years and her bones reburied closer to the house. We arranged to return on Friday when we would visit Ghi's mother's village and family for Huyen to say her farewells there, too.

On Wednesday we finally got Huyen's visa which, to our surprise, was for a period of just over five years, much longer than the twelve months we had been expecting. At the Thai Airways office our luck seemed to have changed as a seat miraculously appeared for Huyen on the evening flight to Bangkok. At last, things seemed to be going to plan, or so we thought! We spent Wednesday and Thursday relaxing as far as was possibly and doing some local shopping. John arranged to have a suit made, something he had always regretted not doing before but the intense heat put me off making any similar purchase for myself. Having fittings when I was so hot and sweaty in the humidity of Hanoi was not something I relished! Ellie agreed to have her fringe cut in the hairdresser's opposite our hotel, turning the tables on Huyen for 2004! We also bought matching Vietnamese costumes for the twins, red silk tunics with white trousers and then spent a long time finding embroidered slippers to match.

Finally, Friday dawned and we were woken at an incredibly early hour by workmen immediately next to our bedroom demolishing the next door property with jackhammers. John was not amused and stormed out in his pyjamas to confront them. The language barrier was not a problem. They understood exactly what he was saying from his posture and tone of voice and the noise stopped for the next hour or so! Anh arrived in a taxi and we were at Vu Duong by 10am, leaving almost immediately for Ghi's mother's village, a journey of around one and a half hours, with Son, Ghi and Huyen on board. The air was oppressively hot and humid when we left the taxi's air-conditioned atmosphere to walk around two sides of the large rectangular pond in which appeared to be growing a variety of watercress. On our previous visit in 2004 heavy rain had flooded this path and the family had put out duck-boards for us to walk along. We had arrived too late to eat with them since they always eat early as their day begins so much earlier than ours. We feasted in the room we remembered from 2004, coping well even with the chopsticks. There were more speeches and both girls were given a silver chain necklace as a present. We promised to maintain contact and finally left at 2.30pm after John had taken a host of photographs. We dropped the family back home but did not stop ourselves. A quiet evening and an early night since we knew how traumatic tomorrow would probably be.

Saturday and the final day when Ghi and Son would hold their farewell party. We delayed our arrival at the village until 10.30am to keep an emotional day as short as possible. We recognised many of the lunchtime dishes put before us as we sat with Son and both his half brothers at the little coffee table. Afterwards, another family member arrived, chairman of the village committee which had just received a grant to build a children's playground in the village. We used the taxi to visit the site but it became increasingly obvious that he was hoping for a donation from us. On our return to the house, his interest in us soon evaporated and he quickly left with no goodbyes. At 1.30pm, friends of Son's arrived in two groups with envelopes containing money for Huyen and speeches were made as these were handed over. An hour later, Ghi's friends arrived and the same procedure was followed. In all cases the money was in identical airmail envelopes and although containing thousands of dong amounted to very little in real terms although, to them, the gifts were doubt-lessly significant. Also present were many children who had failed to view our incredible singing performance(!) on Tuesday so we were again thrust into the spotlight. This time we expanded to two songs, adding *There Was An Old Woman Who Swallowed A Fly* to our *Old Macdonald Had A Farm* repertoire (with Anh translating) and felt we had given good value for money! Everyone present wanted Ellie to give a small speech about her feelings, something that could not have been more traumatic for her. Eventually she was persuade to say a few words via Anh to the effect that she was pleased Huyen was coming to England to study, that she had enjoyed seeing everyone here and that it would be nice to have someone to play with but she wished it wasn't so hot! Laughter and applause from the assembled multitude!

At 3.15pm it was time for us to leave, taking Huyen's pathetically few belongings with us in a little suitcase. It was obvious how upset Ghi was. If today was bad then surely tomorrow would be many times worse when we all met up at Noi Bai airport.

Back at the hotel we repacked Huyen's things in our cases so that nothing would get broken. I found it hard to believe how little she had brought. Just about everything amounted to the clothes we had brought from England, virtually no possessions of her own which I found incredibly sad. The money she had been given was also there and from six separate groups amounted to the Vietnamese equivalent of £3.50! We spent a quiet evening – again wondering what tomorrow would bring.

Our last day, an evening flight and several hours to worry about whether Huyen would turn up at the airport or not. John and I both had our doubts. Our goodbyes would be very traumatic since we had bowed to a request and hired a coach to carry all the family members who would be seeing Huyen off. Our hopes of a quiet goodbye to just

Ghi and Son would not materialise so the pressure would be on us all. We arrived far too early at the airport and spent an anxious forty minutes thinking Huyen was not going to appear. At last we saw the bus arrive and disgorge a large number of people – all relatives and close family friends both adults and children. It was highly likely that the majority of the younger ones (especially) had never been out of the village before.

We still had a long wait which was rather awkward since no-one – them or us – really knew what to say. Several of the family were tearful as was expected and understandable. Son and Ghi were effusive in their thanks to us for giving Huyen this chance to 'better herself' and were telling her to 'work hard and obey John and Anne'. For ourselves, we just could not begin to imagine being in their shoes and saying goodbye to Ellie. It was the most moving experience that either of us had ever had and we both desperately wanted the departure gate to open so that we could isolate ourselves from this heart-wrenching situation.

After what seemed to be an incredibly long time our desk was opened. John went forward and was first in the queue but it quickly became apparent that there was a problem of sorts. He was asked to wait to one side whilst all the other passengers were processed and had their luggage weighed through. John was becoming increasingly frustrated by the absence of explanation although he was beginning to suspect that the previous problem at the Thai Airways office had not been resolved in a satisfactory way. He demanded to see 'someone in authority' and the airport manager eventually appeared. It was eventually explained to him that, although Huyen had seats on both legs of the two flights home, the rest of us had, somehow, been taken out of the system – presumably by the woman who had given us Huyen's ticket at the Thai Airways office. According to the computer, we no longer existed – despite the fact that John was clutching the return tickets we had flown out with from London Heathrow!

At first we were told that there were no seats anywhere for us. Then it seemed that there could be seats to Bangkok but not on to London. John was understandably furious. The situation had been created by the incompetence of the airline's own staff. Our anxiety was obvious to all those who were aware of the problem and, no doubt, it was being transmitted to the thirty or so family members who were all waiting around to wave us off and probably not fully understanding the nature of the hold-up. Time ticked on and our anxiety grew as the scheduled departure time rapidly approached. It seemed increasingly likely that the flight would leave without us. The rest of the passengers had long since disappeared through to the departure lounge yet our luggage had still not been processed and put through. We were keen to be on our way since the delay was causing more heartache for everyone, especially Ghi and Son. If necessary, we were prepared to wait in Bangkok until seats for London were available but John reasoned that this was unlikely unless and until we could be restored to the computer system.

Finally, seemingly just a few minutes before the flight was due to depart, the officials told us that London had cleared our seats and we could go. It was then a mad scramble to check in our cases and say a quick goodbye to everyone – Anh, Son, Ghi, Phuong, Nam and all the family members. After two hours of standing around and waiting we were now leaving with indecent haste. We had emotional hugs with Ghi and Son – John making a final and very public exhortation to Son to look after and cherish Ghi and to make sure the older children pulled their weight around the house – and then the four of us hurried through to customs. Amazingly, Huyen had come with us without so much as a backward glance towards her parents. Our passports were dealt with at the inevitable slow pace that we were now so used to whilst John and I imagined that, even now, the plane might take off without us. There was one final moment of amusement on our part as the officials did a double take on seeing both Ellie and Huyen together, one with a British passport and the other with a Vietnamese but both showing the same date of birth. A final turn, a wave to those family members clustered in the doorway, and we were off to the departure lounge at the run – frustratingly having to miss the very inexpensive duty-free shop on the way. We were the last to board.

The Hanoi-Bangkok part of the journey passed quite quickly with the novelty of everything around us. Communication with Huyen was extremely difficult but there were no major problems. We had a very short stop-over in Bangkok, just time to buy some duty free items – and a soft toy picked out by Huyen – plus a drink before we were required to board the London flight. Our first problems began during this second leg when Huyen was unable to eat any of the airline food and obviously felt very lonely and unhappy. At one point she began to cry quietly but we had no idea if she was experiencing travel sickness or was simply unhappy. John hit on the idea of asking if any of the crew spoke Vietnamese but, of course, they were all Thais on this leg of the journey. He then asked if there were any Vietnamese-speaking passengers on board and finally a very pleasant Vietnamese man appeared, travelling with his wife and son. We attempted to explain the situation to him and he had a quiet chat with Huyen. He then explained to us that there was no real problem but that she felt a little sick and homesick which was only to be expected. He returned again during the flight to check on her which was a really thoughtful gesture.

Finally, we landed at a cold and wet Heathrow at 6.30am to be met by Gill and Rod who were waiting for us at the barrier and who we were delighted to see. A situation reminiscent of 1996! After a long, two-hour drive back to Weston-super-Mare – during which Huyen was suddenly very sick all over me – we arrived back at Elmsleigh Road wondering what on earth we had done. She was by then in a very sorry state and the weather was so cold we even turned on the central heating, an unknown event for June! At noon Huyen made a quick phone call home and I was amazed how short she kept it and how unemotional she seemed able to be.

30

And Now We Are Four

John

The first few weeks were a steep learning curve for all of us, especially Huyen. Anne's housekeeping bill rose alarmingly as she strove to find food that Huyen was comfortable eating and every mealtime became an anxiety for the cook. Anne had been advised to keep Huyen's diet very simple to begin with, grilled meat and vegetables only, but there were also many vegetables that she would not eat in Vietnam. Very quickly she showed Anne (and Ellie) how to fry rice in a manner she was familiar with – once we had purchased some fish sauce. Not a smell the rest of us were comfortable with but the resulting dish was quite tasty and even Ellie began to enjoy it. As her staple food, Huyen was keen to eat rice at every meal although we drew a line at breakfast! Most of the foods we ate were alien to her especially dairy products which played little part in a Vietnamese diet.

Despite Anne's misgivings, Huyen began to fill out, putting on weight with the extra calories our Western diet carried. Ice cream and cream were soon favourites although cheese is something she still only tolerates. Today, her diet is fairly cosmopolitan although spicy foods do not interest her or Ellie.

Gradually Huyen began to settle into her new life in a foreign country where everything from the food she ate to the bed she slept in to the language she heard were new experiences which, in fact, she seemed to take in her stride. At first, Huyen clung to Ellie as if she was a Siamese twin and wanted to be in her sister's room whenever possible. Ellie soon began to resent this invasion of her space. After almost twelve years as an only child she was very proprietorial of that space and there were signs that Ellie was beginning to regret Huyen's presence on occasions. She confided that although she liked having a sister she sometimes hankered for the previous status quo with only the three of us. However, the introduction of a few simple ground rules improved things enormously and both girls agreed to knock before going into each others room – even if that soon became just a verbal "knock, knock". It was probably nine months before we began to see a big improvement in their relationship and the mutual benefits that gave both of them.

Simple things like seeing them, heads together, watching a DVD or shrieking with laughter at a shared joke; watching them play ball together in the garden or walking to the paper shop to collect sweets and a newspaper. These are memories that we can store away and remember when a heated argument is taking place or one or the other has dissolved into tears! Probably no worse than any sibling disagreements but, of course, we have no yardstick to measure them by.

The biggest challenge we faced was adapting to being a family of four from three. The new configuration was particularly hard on Ellie who had suddenly to come to terms with the fact that she was no longer an only child at the centre of the family. Of course, a first-born in any family has a lot of adjusting to cope with when a younger sibling or siblings arrive but the older child has many months to come to terms with the prospect of a new arrival and a baby is quite different to a ready made sibling of the same or similar age. With the constant attention Huyen inevitably received, Anne and I began to worry that Ellie might start to think that her place in the family had been lost to her twin.

We strove to show her how much we loved her but there were occasional arguments and tensions within the home as well as between the two girls. It was a difficult situation for us all since Huyen was not our daughter and never will be and yet she was enjoying the same lifestyle and 'privileges' that came with the position. An uneasy six months followed made all the more difficult by my Mayoral duties but devastatingly so by the sudden and unexpected stroke I suffered on 2nd July, only six weeks after Huyen's arrival. Knowing that Huyen would need constant company, I had retired from my second career as a solicitor and, most importantly, was transporting her three times a week to the private English lessons that we had arranged with Sue Southwell, the English-to-foreign-students language teacher who lived three miles away in the village of Bleadon. Although I made a speedy recovery (thanks in part to my determination to greet the Queen and Prince Philip who were due to visit Weston at the end of the month for the first time in thirty years), hospital tests indicated that my vision had been slightly affected in the upper-left quadrant. However, as far as I was concerned, this problem did not adversely affect my ability and competence to drive a car since the area concerned was above the level of the top of the windscreen.

September and the start of the twin's first term at Sidcot

School ten miles away saw me entering into a lift-share arrangement with another family but, almost immediately, I got cold feet at the thought that my insurance might be invalidated if I was involved in an accident, whether it was my fault or not, and a problem with my eyes became known. The arrangement was straightaway changed with the other family doing the morning run and Anne now doing the return trip home in the evening. This was not at all what we had originally intended but this new schedule worked reasonably well.

Huyen had started at Sidcot with just forty five hours of English lessons with Sue but, of course, she was living in an English-speaking household and was therefore surrounded by this new language during all her waking hours. The only Vietnamese she spoke was on a Sunday morning when her family traipsed along to an internet café on the outskirts of their village and were able to speak to Huyen via a Skype link and she and they could see each other courtesy of an inexpensive webcam at either end. This forty minute contact each week certainly helped to maintain her link with her family. What a wonderful facility Skype is. Free to download at Skype.com and one can then speak to anyone in the world for anything up to an hour at absolutely no cost whatsoever.

However, as the months wore on, I began to have doubts about the wisdom of what we had done. At a fairly early stage, Huyen had asked Anne if she could call us Mum and Dad rather than Anne and John. Caught somewhat off guard, Anne had agreed without discussing it with me and I was subsequently unsure that she had made the right decision. I was concerned that Huyen might start to compare her life in Vietnam unfavourably with her new life in England and shift her focus from her birth family onto us. This seemed to be a realistic concern when, a few months later, we discovered that Huyen had told her parents that she would, in future, speak to them every other Sunday rather than weekly. We instantly put a stop to that and insisted that she re-establish the previous arrangement.

As the first twelve months went by, I began to have other concerns about the wisdom of what we were doing. Huyen had a five-year visa to study in the UK and there was every likelihood that she would stay on afterwards to study A levels and, perhaps, go on to university. However, would this send her back to Vietnam in her early twenties with, hopefully, impressive Western qualifications but with only a twelve-year old's vocabulary in her native language and without any basic knowledge of her own country's history, geography, heritage and customs *et cetera*. Anne agreed that this was certainly a very real problem but what to do for the best?

I discussed the matter with Anh in a series of emails and she, in turn, sounded out Son and Ghi. Slightly to our surprise, they were quite sure that it was in Huyen's best interests to stay in England for as long as possible and, indeed, they suggested that she should not return to Vietnam to visit them at the end of the summer term as had been originally arranged. That, in itself, had been an increasing worry for us as we were not at all comfortable with her travelling care of the cabin crew but neither did we relish the prospect of the time and expense of accompanying her to Hanoi and returning some six weeks later to collect her again. Fortunately, Anh's son, Tuan, was (and still is) living and working in London after finishing his degree course at Imperial College and it was highly likely that he or one of his Vietnamese friends could and would be able to accompany Huyen as they returned to visit their own families. Huyen was not aware of any of these thoughts and discussions unless they were communicated to her by her parents in one of their weekly chats.

Eventually, I consulted Ellie as Anne and I both felt that her opinion was a vital ingredient. She carefully thought about the situation and then explained that although having Huyen around was a problem for her from time to time she would not want her to return to Vietnam permanently. What had started out for Ellie as an adventure had palled slightly with the constant presence of someone who copied everything she did, often repeated what she said and who, far too often, invaded her space but had become the norm. Ellie admitted – perhaps to herself for the first time – that she would miss Huyen if she were to return home and the downside of having a near look-a-like twin was by far out-weighed by the company and the love that had developed between them.

So that was that!

Having a twin was a source of both vexation and joy to Ellie. She has undoubtedly matured considerably since Huyen's arrival and has learnt many of life's lessons that can sometimes by-pass an only child. She no longer seems so demonstratively loving towards us as she once used to be but that may be more to do with the passage of time than the presence of her sister.

Huyen continued to adapt to her new life with remarkable speed. Her spoken English improved exponentially and is now quite good although she still tends to chop the end off some words which seems to be 'a Vietnamese thing'. (We recall Hanh Tuong in Weston once telling us about her 'knee' and our puzzlement was only relieved a minute or two later when it became apparent that she had been referring to her niece).

Huyen is developing a widening vocabulary having

benefited from a total immersion in the English language at home and at school. We are constantly able to correct her mistakes and she has picked up many of Ellie's phrases and mannerisms. In fact, on the phone, it is not always easy to tell them apart. Her written work is further behind but Anne has spent many hours in the holidays using English grammar books for younger children to improve it. Her school reports have all been excellent – her teachers commending her for her excellent effort in every subject – showing her to be a child who wants to succeed and is determined to do so. She is much more sporty than Ellie something, I believe, that stems from the type of play she was used to with her friends in Vietnam. I remember in the first few weeks how she showed us a primitive shuttle-cock she had made from a ball of paper, a few feathers and a thick rubber band. She was capable of keeping this airborne for a considerable time using only her feet whilst Anne could only manage two consecutive touches!

Another adaptation which we both find a little sad but which, I guess, is only inevitable, has been the speed with which she has accepted Western ideas and values and she is currently desperate to have her first mobile phone!

It was fun passing through the many milestones that punctuate our calendar year: the first birthday, showing Huyen a typical English Christmas, writing a letter to Santa, an introduction to the Tooth Fairy and many more things when she would look to Ellie for a lead. This occasionally led to an exasperated Ellie who sometimes felt she was losing her individuality as Huyen was so keen to copy her!

As anticipated, one of the greatest problems we have encountered has been in the way we treat the twins together and individually. Having given only a passing thought to this before Huyen arrived, I can see how naïve we were not to have considered it more fully. Should Huyen be treated exactly the same as Ellie or should Ellie, by right of being our daughter, have any extra privileges? A classic example of this eventually arose over mobile phones. Ellie already had one for emergency purposes so that she could contact us if she suddenly had an after-school activity and needed to be picked up earlier or later than was usual. In due course, Huyen also wanted one but we decided that she could use Ellie's, if-and-when necessary. With only one salary coming into the house together with a modest pension and two sets of school fees to pay out, we have to manage the twins' expectations on several fronts. They have to learn that they will not always be able to have what some of their more affluent friends have. It is a lesson that we all have to learn at some stage or other in our lives. However, in the vast majority of cases and at all major events such as birthdays and Christmas, Ellie and Huyen are treated in exactly the same way which, of course, is exactly as it should be.

As for expressions of affection, we are a demonstrative family but kissing appears to be something that Huyen is not used to and is, possibly, uncomfortable with. So, whereas Ellie comes to us for a goodnight kiss every evening Huyen simply puts her head round the door for an exchange of goodnights. However, both girls like Anne to follow them to their bedrooms for a final goodnight and a tuck-in. One exception to Huyen's reluctance to kiss is Grandma who she readily embraces alongside Ellie.

Once the joint decision had been made that Huyen would continue her stay with us we both felt an enormous sense of relief after the trauma of the past months. But, it was unfortunate that we were then unable to celebrate the end of our busy Mayoral year with a long-awaited holiday by another unforeseen problem associated with Huyen. It

265

was two years since we had last visited France and we had just begun looking into travel arrangements for a visit that summer, 2008. We suddenly discovered that Huyen would need a visa as she would be travelling on a Vietnamese passport. We originally assumed that since Huyen would be travelling with us as our ward and as Ellie's twin her somewhat unique situation would be viewed sympathetically by the French authorities. But no. The United Kingdom had not signed up to one of the European Conventions and as a result Huyen would need something called a Schengen visa. OK, we would apply for one – but then discovered that this would entail a face-to-face interview at the French Embassy in London and such interviews had to be arranged in advance. Moreover, a visa could not be issued more than two months prior to departure. The whole process would entail Huyen and I spending the best part of a day travelling to and from the French Embassy by train or coach since I was still not allowed to drive. Huyen would, of course, have to miss a whole day's school into the bargain. It seemed to be a frustratingly bureaucratic system for a twelve year old child to have to go through.

So, we tried to get into the French Embassy's system – which entailed pre-booking on their internet site. But appointments could not be made more than thirty two days ahead and the site was fully booked to that limit. We were advised that cancellations were advertised every Thursday morning but although I sat in front of the computer all morning for several Thursdays, no cancellations appeared. I tried sending pleading emails explaining that the person requiring the visa was a twelve year old family member but only ever received standard copies of the Embassy's system and requirements in reply. Eventually, there was not enough of the school summer holiday left and we had to abandon all hopes of getting away. This was rather galling since the weather at home had been appalling through late July and all of August and we had, in effect, not had any holiday whatsoever. This was particularly disappointing for Anne who was faced with the prospect of a return to the rigours of another school year without the chance to recharge her batteries.

The only good news came from the DVLA with the renewal of my driving licence following yet another eye test. The school runs starting in early September for the twins' second year at Sidcot would now be much easier and I suddenly had far more control over my life and could look forward to doing some of those things that had been earmarked for my retirement years.

Huyen's second year at Sidcot spanning 2008/9 ran far more smoothly as school was not such an unknown quantity for her. Her spoken English had advanced with considerable skill (although the written language, under-standably, was lagging behind somewhat) and both girls had settled into strong friendship patterns with a group of four or five other girls with at least two of them as special friends. Their twelfth birthday was celebrated with a huge sleepover, quite different from the quiet occasion the year before.

After Christmas, we knew that we would need to think about arranging Huyen's return visit to her family in the summer, 2009. We explored the possibility of her travelling with Tuan or one of his Vietnamese friends in London but if any of them were travelling, the dates did not fit. However, using Tuan's previous experience of accompanied travel with Singapore Airlines and an agency he put us in touch with, comforting arrangements were soon put in place for Huyen to travel to and from Hanoi care of airline staff. She would leave from Heathrow three days after Sidcot School broke up for the summer holiday on 6th July, spend nine weeks with her family and we would meet her again at Heathrow a few days after the autumn term began again in early September.

The next five months moved forward quickly with Huyen starting her periods, closely followed by Ellie. Anne was amazed since she had always assumed that their small size would make them late developers. Certainly, some of their bigger friends had yet to reach this milestone but Anne was to learn that Ghi had also been thirteen when she started. Genes must play a significant part in this process.

We had made no plans for the summer holiday but were quite content that we would be able to organise such matters at the last moment now that we had no need to arrange a visa for Huyen if we decided to hop on a ferry to France. Additionally, we had a loose invitation to visit some French friends who live at Carnac in Brittany. July seemed to be upon us all too quickly and we were suddenly rushing around to find last-minute presents for Huyen to take back for members of her family. She was obviously very excited about going but understandably more than a little apprehensive about undertaking such a long flight on her own – especially with its stop-over in Singapore where she would be changing planes. No doubt Son, Ghi and her half sister and brothers were counting the days, too. Ellie, slightly surprisingly, was not looking forward to a summer on her own – a huge turnaround from her attitude the previous year when she might have welcomed some solitude. This was more evidence of the twins' growing and closer relationship.

Although we would miss Huyen, as parents we were really looking forward to a summer of being just the three of us and having Ellie to ourselves again. We both hoped that we could recapture some of the closeness that we had known previously but, perhaps, that had been lost forever. It may be that it was a natural progression to do more with age than the presence of Huyen in our family unit.

The end of term arrived all too quickly and Ellie and I set out at 8am the following Tuesday to take Huyen to Heathrow airport. However, just a few miles up the M5 the exhaust fell off my somewhat ancient car on Tickenham Hill and I had to pull into the Gordano Services at Junction 19 to phone Anne to bring her car for the rest of the journey. A not-too-pleased Anne arrived, swopped cars and returned to school in mine whilst I renewed my journey eastwards in hers. The trip was otherwise uneventful and we arrived in good time to book Huyen in for her lunchtime flight.

At this point it was explained to me that Huyen, together with a group of seven or eight other children, would be accompanied by and closely supervised by a member of the airline's ground staff before being handed over to cabin crew. During the flight they would be looked after by the crew before being handed over to ground staff again at Singapore. This process would be repeated until Huyen would, eventually, be handed over to her parents at Noi Bai airport – but only on their signature! The same process would be repeated on her eventual return flights when I would have to sign for her on production of my passport as proof of identity. What a wonderful system and it was clear to see that any worries Huyen may have had had completely disappeared.

To our surprise, two days later, we had a very brief early morning phone call from Huyen to let us know that she had just arrived safely at the family house in Vu Duong.

Anne
John and Ellie returned alone. I do not think that Ellie could quite believe how much she was going to miss her

sister and for several days she was like a lost soul. Life, however, soon settled into a pattern and we both tried to give Ellie that extra attention to help her come to terms with being an only child again. The girls had arranged to chat on a Skype link every Sunday morning but usually either the link or the camera was not working at the other end and the twins had to resort to typing backwards and forwards via the computer.

For us, it was a wonderful summer punctuated by several short visits to relatives in parts of the country we had not previously been to and culminating in a very enjoyable fortnight with Didier and Vony, our French friends in Brittany. The weather was good, we were able to relax, swim, read and play numerous games of Ellie's favourite card game. We were also able to impress her with our ability to sustain two weeks of conversations in French with our friends – something that may be a spur for Ellie to work at overcoming her natural shyness before living *en famille* next year as part of a short stay in France on an annual school visit. It was the break we all needed after a long and difficult two years.

John

All too soon the holidays were over and school had started again. There was a lurking thought that Huyen might not come back but we eventually had confirmation that she was on her way and I met her again at London Heathrow (and signed for her on production of my passport) at an early hour a few days after term had started.

She was tired after such a long flight and, of course, was experiencing an eight-hour time difference. She had a short weep as we got into the car and another a few miles down the M4 so I resisted the temptation to ask her about her visit home. That could wait until she had settled back into her routine in England.

Huyen was sufficiently alert to be able to go to school for the afternoon session and Ellie and her various friends were surprised and delighted to suddenly see her arrive in the dining hall. Everything was 'back to normal'.

31

And Finally...

Well, not finally finally, really, since this is a whole life story that has, hopefully, many decades to run. The story of two babies who were being separated from one another and might never have known of each other's existence if we had not appeared at just the right moment. The story of the twins has arisen so many times on a variety of occasions such as dinner parties and it is still very easy to become quite emotional during the telling of their story. On many of those occasions, people have said, "Oh, what a lovely story. You should write a book" and, eventually, we thought that we would. And here it is. It started out as – and predominately still is – Ellie's story but, after Ghi's letter in 2004, it became Huyen's story, too.

However, even that is not entirely correct. Of course, it is not just the twins' story. It is our story as well – one which has covered the passage of over twenty years. Last March, the Daily Telegraph reported that France's first lady, Carla Bruni-Sarkozy, intends to adopt a baby if she cannot have one with her husband, President Nicholas Sarkozy. The 41 year old singer and former model told the French magazine, Le Figaro, "If it's not biologically possible, I'll adopt one. Adoption is perhaps the purest form of mother-hood." She added, "I'm not obsessed by blood ties. I think you can build a powerful bond without that."

We would agree absolutely with that sentiment. Ellie has enriched our lives beyond all anticipation from the very first moment we took her back to our hotel room in Hanoi at the end of January 1996 as a three-month old little mite weighing just 6lbs 'wringing wet'.

She has never seen herself as anything other than our child and we suspect that she never will. She is growing up with a true sense of her own identity and it seems quite unremarkable that she identifies with everything British. She is a very intelligent child with an enquiring mind and is an avid reader. We kept our promise, given entirely of our own volition, to maintain her links with her birth family and she need never wonder what her twin would be like since she now has first-hand knowledge.

What the future will bring for Huyen will be a case of 'wait and see'. Whether we should have 'meddled' or not by bringing her to England, we will probably never know, but it seemed to be the right thing to do once we had received Ghi's 2004 letter. Our motive was, as has already been said, to give Ghi the chance to escape from a seemingly unhappy marriage. The fact that she has not done so would seem to suggest that we were misled. However, we hope that Huyen will be a source of pride to her parents and that her command of the English language and her secondary education in England will, eventually, be used to the family's benefit since, we hope and expect, she will be able to gain well-paid employment back in Hanoi that will have the potential to benefit them all. Perhaps that will even allow other members of the family to visit Ellie in England.

* * *

If we could put the clock back, would we do it all again?

Without the shadow of a doubt! And maybe our story will encourage other childless couples to follow their dream. It won't be easy but everything is possible if you are sufficiently determined to succeed. The rewards are unbelievable.